Smithian Morals

Smithian Morals takes up Adam Smith's thought on justice, virtue, propriety, beneficialness, liberty, God, and the conscience. Smith is pursued as exemplar, sage, moral guide, and therapist. Smith teaches us to think dialectically. At the center of Smith's thought Klein sees a robust affirmation: "allowing every man to pursue his own interest his own way, upon the liberal plan of equality, liberty, and justice." Smith teaches a presumption of liberty. The strength of that presumption is up to us. Smith's liberalism is outspoken to the point of abolitionism on particular issues, but in a broader sense it is conservative; it is an engaging, humane conservative liberalism. It emanates from a true moralist and his philosophy of virtue. Smith teaches a presumption of liberty not from first principles or purportedly self-evident propositions. He picks up midstream, mindful of the waters about all he treats and the waters about his own weather-beaten vessel, for he is coursing upon the waters with us. As interpreter of Smith's texts, Klein is open about his tendencies toward classical liberalism, non-foundationalism, and esoteric reading.

About the author:

Daniel Klein is professor of economics and JIN Chair at the Mercatus Center at George Mason University, where, with Erik Matson and Don Boudreaux, he leads a program in Adam Smith. He is also research fellow at the Ratio Institute (Stockholm) and chief editor of *Econ Journal Watch*. With Matson, he also co-director of CL Press and the Adam Smith Works/Liberty Fund monthly feature Just Sentiments.

On Dan Klein's scholarship on Adam Smith

Richard Whatmore, Professor and Chair of Modern History, University of St. Andrews, editor of *History of European Ideas*, and Co-direct of St. Andrews Institute of Intellectual History:

> "In 2023 Adam Smith will be 300 years old. There will be a very large number of ill-informed books about him being published in this special year. Smith—now that we are recovering the actual historical Smith—still has a great deal to say to us. Dan Klein knows this, understands Smith as well as any scholar and has a gift for communicating (understatement). Everything he publishes is accessible and significant. It is also worth saying that his public presence is remarkable and remarkably wide-ranging. He reaches audiences fellow academics simply cannot reach."

Deirdre Nansen McCloskey, Distinguished Professor Emerita of Economics and of History, and Professor Emerita of English and of Communication, adjunct in classics and philosophy, at the University of Illinois at Chicago:

> "Klein is the rare economist who listens to what others say. In this he follows Smith, and with these volumes emerges as the sage's leading listener. He writes beautifully and with purpose, to bring us away from the Smith of left or right coercion and towards the Smith of what he calls "spiral," a vein of the Scottish enlightenment, and still therapeutic for our own troubled times."

Knud Haakonssen, Long-term Fellow at the Max Weber Centre for Advanced Cultural and Social Studies, University of Erfurt, Professor of Intellectual History, University of St. Andrews and Co-direct of St. Andrews Institute of Intellectual History, and General Editor of the Liberty Fund book series Natural Law and Enlightenment Classics.

> "Dan Klein's collection of papers represents an imposing body of work on Smith as an historical figure and as thinker of lasting relevance. The papers have an impressive range, which is what Smith's many-sided work requires. At the same time, there is a keen engagement with the scholarly and critical literature. Klein's writing is clear and direct. It is a pleasure to recommend the collection."

Vernon Smith, Nobel laureate in Economics and Professor, Smith Institute for Political Economy and Philosophy, Chapman University:

> "Three centuries after his birth, Adam Smith was never more relevant and inspiring. Dan Klein's essays convey that inspiration in an accessible style reinforcing the relevance of this greatest of 18th century scholars."

Thomas W. Merrill, Associate Professor, Department of Government, American University, Director of Special Programs at the Political Theory Institute, American University:

> "Dan Klein has long been constructing a portrait of Adam Smith in his complexity—moving back and forth in a deepening spiral between Smith's policy recommendations, his rich phenomenology of ethical life, and even his reflections on our place in the cosmos. With this

collection we can now see the richness of Klein's reading of Smith in synoptic view, both in the specificity of its parts and in the vision that animates the whole. Klein is a spirited and skilled advocate for liberalism in its original political sense. He sheds light on the presumption of liberty, the structure of justice, the spiraling complexity of ethical life, the subtlety of Smith's rhetoric, and Smith's religion. This work will be helpful to readers just coming to know Smith for the first time, and it certainly deserves the attention of scholars of Smith and of the history of liberalism. It enriches our sense of Smith even as we argue with it. It is an achievement worth celebrating."

Douglas Den Uyl, Vice President of Educational Programs, Liberty Fund:

"Dan Klein is one of the most distinctive and thorough interpreters of Adam Smith working today. His insights into Smith are both instructive and compelling. It is of immense value to have many of these insights collected together, especially because so many of them are accessible to the scholar and general intelligent reader alike."

Peter Minowitz, Professor of Political Science, Santa Clara University and author of *Profits, Priests, and Princes: Adam Smith's Emancipation of Economics from Politics and Religion*:

"An economist with abiding interests in public policy, Klein has developed an acute appreciation of how carefully Adam Smith wrote—and of how comprehensively he thought. Klein manifests a rare combination of virtues, and they are especially valuable in our world, which struggles to balance economic and non-economic goods. The precision and efficiency of Klein's prose, furthermore, provide a fitting tribute to Smith. More importantly, they should inspire—and even equip—us to counteract the literary degradations associated with tweeting and partisan hyperbole."

James Otteson, Professor of Business Ethics, University of Notre Dame, and author of *Adam Smith's Marketplace of Life* (Cambridge, 2002), *Actual Ethics* (Cambridge, 2006), *Adam Smith* (Bloomsbury, 2013), *The End of Socialism* (Cambridge, 2014), *Honorable Business: A Framework for Business in a Just and Humane Society* (Oxford, 2019):

"Adam Smith is one of the most widely cited and least read great figures in the West. He is often pressed into the service of contemporary authors' ends without sufficient regard for the breadth, depth, subtlety, and sophistication of his work. Daniel Klein's essays provide an important corrective. Klein combines close reading of Smith with a critical yet charitable eye, helping us understand both the details in Smith's work and its larger aims, and, in the process, showing why Smith deserves a place in the pantheon of great philosophers. Those new to Smith may be astonished at the range and penetration of Smith's insights revealed by Klein's essays. Even Smith scholars will find much that is new, enlightening, and challenging. This collection provides a rich resource for philosophers, economists, historians, and anyone else interested in one of the great observers of human behavior."

Smithian Morals

Daniel B. Klein

CL Press

Published by CL PRESS
A project of the Fraser Institute
1770 Burrard Street, 4th Floor
Vancouver, BC V6J 3G7 Canada
www.clpress.net

Smithian Morals
Daniel B. Klein

© 2023 by CL Press

ISBN: 978-1-957698-02-1

Cover design by John Stephens
Interior layout by Joanna Andreasson

Searchable PDF of this entire book, with colors in figures,
open access, free:
https://clpress.net/

Contents

Preface

This volume consists of short chapters derived from short pieces that I and sometimes coauthors (Erik Matson, Kendra Asher, Michael Clark) wrote about Adam Smith and Smithian morals. The pieces have been revised somewhat, notably to reduce repetitiveness.

Three centuries after his birth, does it make sense for you, the Reader, to read the present essays about Adam Smith?

The human soul shall not be captured in words. Souls relate to souls, using signs such as words. Souls relate to souls by shared experience, shared history, shared cultural referents. Human creatures of 2023 started by relating to others in the flesh, notably mother and father, and, only by some progression, do they work their way back in time to others.

The pieces collected here dabble in intellectual history, but the larger aim is to explore what it is we should think, feel, believe, say. When I say "Adam Smith thought X about Y," I usually am also saying, "We should think X about Y." Smith is here a supposed mentor, sage, exemplar, with whom we have an encounter, or even maintain a sort of friendship. Communing with Smith is supposed here to be a way to make better sense of Y. Also supposed is that we seek perennially to make better sense.

Acknowledgments

Of the 28 chapters here, 14 derive directly from articles published by Liberty Fund—eleven from *Adam Smith Works*, two from *Law & Liberty*, and one from *Liberty Matters*. I am grateful to Amy Willis, Sarah Skwire, Doug Den Uyl, Christy Horpedahl, and others at Liberty Fund who have supported my writings there. (Among the pieces appearing originally at *Adam Smith Works*, three appeared in the feature there *Just Sentiments*, which Erik Matson and I curate.) Among the other 14 chapters, the original incarnations appeared at *City Journal* (Manhattan Institute) (ch. 3), *The Independent Review* (chs. 7 and 23) and The Beacon (ch.27) (Independent Institute), Bet On It (Bryan Caplan) (ch. 21), the Institute of Economic Affairs (chs. 19 and 22), the American Institute for Economic Research (ch. 21), the Foundation for Economic Education (chs. 10 and 15), the American Enterprise Institute (ch. 4), *Svensk Tidskrift* (ch. 16), and the Oxford University Press blog (ch. 28). I am grateful to them for their support.

I thank coauthors of works from which five of the chapters derive, Erik Matson, Kendra Asher, Michael Clark, and Caroline Breashears (who instructed me not to list her as coauthor of the portion of our 2022 *Economic Affairs* article used here in Chapter 22). I thank Jacob Hall for helping to put this book together at the end, and Jane Shaw Stroup for copy-editing the final manuscript. I thank Joanna Andreasson for layout and typesetting the interior, and John Stephens for designing the cover.

Citing Smith's Works

(TMS 263.5) means page 263, paragraph 5 of *The Theory of Moral Sentiments*. Citations to Smith's works are to the Glasgow edition, published by Oxford University Press (1976) and republished by Liberty Fund (1982), listed in the References at the end of this book. The abbreviations are as follows:

TMS–*The Theory of Moral Sentiments*

WN–*The Wealth of Nations*

EPS–*Essays on Philosophical Subjects*

LJ–*Lectures on Jurisprudence*

LRBL–*Lectures on Rhetoric and Belles Lettres*

CHAPTER 1

Benevolence, Beneficence, and Beneficialness

I love to analyze sentiments, sympathies, and virtues. In doing so, it's useful to distinguish several "b" words.

Benevolence on the part of Mary is a sentiment of directed well-wishing toward the objects of her benevolence. We are benevolent toward our neighbors when their trusted aims and interests are our hopes. Benevolence is particularistic. That is, it pays attention to particular people or particular problems.

Beneficence on Mary's part is her rendering benefit from benevolent impulse. Mary's impulse could be, of course, mixed with other sentiments, but the more the impulse is benevolence, the more apt it is to call it beneficence.

By removing the middle characters of "beneficent action" we get *benefaction*, done by a "beneficent actor," or *benefactor*. With beneficence we have a benefactor (Mary) and beneficiaries (the neighbors).

In a section of *The Theory of Moral Sentiments* (TMS) called "Of Justice and Beneficence," Adam Smith contrasts the virtue of beneficence with the virtue of commutative justice. Commutative justice is not messing with other people's stuff, including promises-due. In the exchange of property or services, this virtue calls us merely to do so on voluntary terms of consent and contract.

When you shop at Safeway and exchange your money for their eggs, you benefit. But we would not say that Safeway showed beneficence. It was ordinary exchange and common decency. Common decency and commutative justice of course have a pro-humanity, live-and-let-live spirit to them, but that spirit is not a lively sentiment. Also, the spirit of common decency is not directed toward particular people or particular problems the way that benevolence is. Benevolence enters into situations. Common decency takes a friendly, peaceful stance toward almost all situations, without entering into them deeply. In the Safeway transaction, therefore, the impulse to render the benefit was not benevolence, so Safeway was not being beneficent.

Though not beneficent, Safeway is beneficial. *Beneficialness* is the rendering of net benefits, irrespective of motive or impulse. The big lesson of *The Wealth of Nations* is that in the modern world, for much of the beneficialness we enjoy, we have to rely on impulses and virtues other than benevolence. We're not in the small hunter-gatherer band anymore.

Does Smith use *benevolence, beneficence*, and *beneficialness* along such lines?

The words *benevolence* and *beneficence* are used abundantly by Adam Smith in *The Theory of Moral Sentiments*, along the lines offered here.

Beneficialness was not used in Smith's time. He used *utility* (notably in Part IV), as well as other terms and expressions.

The difference between benevolence and beneficence relates to a difference between the theistic and the non-theistic versions of the ethical plexus in TMS. In the theistic version, the impartial spectator in the highest sense of the term is God. God is benevolent toward the whole of humankind.

I said that benevolence is particularistic in the way it is directed (toward particular people or particular problems), but that's not the case for God, because God is super knowledgeable and, as it were, can focus on all of the particulars of all such things. Like Santa Claus on Christmas Eve, God gets around in a super-human way, and is benevolent at each stop.

But God, again like Santa Claus, is also beneficent—for example, in the act of divine providence. God delivers benefit from benevolent impulse, and hence is beneficent.

In the allegorical but non-theistic version, the impartial spectator in the highest sense of the term is benevolent, and has, like God, super knowledge. But this allegorical universal beholder only need be benevolent. She wants to see humankind happy and flourishing; that is what she finds beautiful, just like God. But her benevolence is not actualized as benefit. This allegorical being, whom I call Joy, is benevolent to the whole of humankind, but we don't necessarily have grounds to say that she is beneficent toward humankind.

In this respect, Joy is to us as we are to a character in a movie, such as Tess McGill in *Working Girl* or the persons endangered in *Chernobyl*. We enter into their situations and feel benevolence, but we do not render benefits to the objects of that benevolence. We are mere spectators.

Beneficence inspires gratitude. One of the many shortcomings of Joy, as compared to God, is that Joy does not easily lend herself as the object of a general gratitude for life and its blessings, since she has not given us life and its blessings. She only has been benevolent. I've written about whether a feeling of gratitude requires that the gratitude be directed *to* some benefactor. I think that a feeling of gratitude for life is a happy and healthy thing. Finding and enjoying that healthy feeling is a greater challenge for non-theists: They may know *what* they feel grateful *for*, but they may not know *whom* to feel grateful *to*.

CHAPTER 2

Propriety in Adam Smith

Deep mysteries inhere in Adam Smith's moral theory, and not least in the idea of propriety. The reader of *The Theory of Moral Sentiments* finds that a sense of propriety operates in every sympathy. Since Smith holds that all moral sentiments relate to a sympathy, that means that all moral sentiments involve a sense of propriety. The reader of TMS encounters many wondrous formulations, and finds, again and again, propriety playing a central role. Indeed, a sense of propriety operates at every sympathetic fold of every formulation. Here I offer some pointers on propriety in Adam Smith.

Propriety as the "OK" region between praiseworthiness and blameworthiness

Suppose we are guests of Jim at a gathering he is hosting at his home. We might judge Jim's efforts in hospitality. Early in TMS (25.7) Smith designates *propriety* as the appellation for the "fair to middling" region between praiseworthiness and blameworthiness. Conduct that exceeds propriety is deemed praiseworthy, and conduct that falls short of propriety is deemed blameworthy. Propriety itself is just "OK," neither praiseworthy nor blameworthy. We have some notions as to the hospitality Jim should show in his intentions and purposes and hence in his efforts and actions—his *conduct*—and if he exceeds those notions we praise his hospitality, and if he falls short, we blame him for failing to show the hospitality properly due.

Smith speaks of a degree "commonly attained" or "commonly arrived at" by those of Jim's station or reference group. In pondering our own conduct, we consider the conduct "which the greater part of our friends and companions, of our rivals and competitors, may have actually arrived at" (TMS 247.23, 248.25). Interpreting "the greater part of men" (TMS 26.8) to mean something like the quality grade or level arrived at by 50 percent of the community or reference group, we have a sort of middle band, or "mere propriety" (TMS 25.7). It is natural to associate propriety with what is average.

As Smith puts it, "The ordinary degree itself seems neither blamable nor praise-worthy" (TMS 80.6). "Whatever goes beyond this degree…seems to deserve applause; and whatever falls short of it, to deserve blame" (TMS 26.9). The more that Jim's conduct exceeds propriety, the more praiseworthy it is, and the more it falls short, the more blameworthy.

FIG. 2.1: PROPRIETY, PRAISEWORTHINESS, AND BLAMEWORTHINESS FOR COMMUNITY J

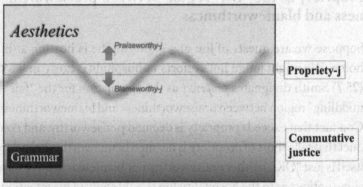

In Figure 2.1 the vertical dimension represents conduct quality. The red, straight, solid line represents the rules of commutative justice; those rules tell you not to mess with other people's stuff.

Commutative justice is singular among the virtues in that its rules are "precise and accurate" (TMS 327.1, 175.11). As compared to the case with other virtues, whether commutative justice has been transgressed is something about which the people within the broad society generally agree.

It is otherwise for the wavy gold lines, or the aesthetic area. There, the particular community or reference group matters. The gold aesthetic area carries an index j, which stands for community j within the broader society. Standards vary by reference groups. What is OK for 10-year-olds is not OK for 30-year-olds; what is good for high school baseball is not good for professional baseball. What is praiseworthy for community j might be just OK for community j+1, and blameworthy for community j+2.

The gold aesthetic rules are sketchy and wavy because, as one checks in among members of community j, arrayed along the horizontal axis, they will return somewhat different ideas of where OK lies. As Smith said, these rules are "loose, vague, and indeterminate" (TMS 175.11, 327.1). But from experience with community j, or after checking around, one can get a sense of the band of propriety.

Propriety is represented as a band, rather than a thin line, because the "OK" range is not necessarily narrow. In practical affairs, propriety is often fuzzy; there is usually some shared sense of what is regarded as "just OK," but often there is no sharply defined, or focal, benchmark. Furthermore, thinking of propriety as a band, rather than as a sharp line, reminds us that moral approval is a matter of gradation, and two instances of conduct that are separated just a little vertically are close in moral approval.

Propriety pertains especially to the "loose, vague, and indeterminate" rules of the becoming virtues—all virtues apart from commutative justice.[1] Commutative justice is very special among the virtues, because its rules are "precise and accurate," or grammar-like, from which a number of special features flow. Among the special features of commutative justice is that feedback on one's conduct with respect to commutative justice is never positive: Grownups don't deserve praise for not messing with other people's stuff, just as they don't deserve praise for getting their grammar right.

Aspects of conduct and 3V-framing

Suppose that we agree that Jim's hospitality falls short of propriety. But still we haven't specified Jim's vice. One common and valuable approach to analyzing a virtue is to consider its salient aspects and see the virtue as lying between deficiency and excess with respect to some such salient aspect. Maybe Jim is inattentive to the physical comfort of his guests. But, instead, maybe he is obsessively attentive. In such framing, proper hospitality lies between indifference and "helicoptering." Smith presents such a frame in discussing Aristotle: "Every particular virtue, according to him, lies in a kind of middle between two opposite vices, of which the one offends from being too much, the other from being too little affected by a particular species of objects" (TMS 270.12), and Smith gives three examples:

Vice of deficiency	Virtue	Vice of excess
cowardice	courage	presumptuous rashness
profusion	frugality	avarice
pusillanimity	magnanimity	arrogance

1. On the neutral feedback due to the practice of commutative justice, Smith says: "There is, no doubt, a propriety in the practice of justice, and it merits, upon that account, all the approbation which is due to propriety" (82.9). But one is well advised to read Smith as suggesting that propriety pertains only to loose, vague, and indeterminate rules, and hence not to commutative justice; see TMS 294.50, 270.11, and 136.3.

Once we have specified a virtue and a salient aspect of it, we have a spectral continuum of *Deficiency-Virtue-Excess*. Thus we have Vice-Virtue-Vice. Call such framing *3V-framing*.

Smith proceeds to embrace 3V-framing: "It is unnecessary to observe that this account of virtue corresponds...pretty exactly with what has been said above concerning the propriety and impropriety of conduct" (TMS 271.12).

Disambiguating (A) propriety as just OK or average and (B) virtue's association with "mediocrity," "middle," and "moderation"

Smith writes about how different passions find an appropriate range of "pitch," neither too "high" nor too "low." This range Smith describes as "a certain mediocrity" (TMS 27.1). In the treatment of Aristotle at pp. 270-271 he likewise uses "mediocrity," "middle," and "moderation." This "mediocrity" is easily confused with propriety, which, as we have seen, corresponds to a "fair to middling" OK, or average degree. But beware not to equate propriety with the Aristotelian "mediocrity" that is depicted in 3V-framing.

Today the term *mediocrity* connotes a lack of excellence, but let's consider cowardice-courage-presumptuous rashness. Figure 2.2 expands on Figure 2.1. On the left-hand slope of Figure 2.2, at which cowardice is separated from courage, a propriety band separates the two. If you look back at Figure 2.1, imagine the word "Courage" replacing the word "Praiseworthy" and the word "Cowardice" replacing the word "Blameworthy."

FIG. 2.2: A VIRTUE LYING BETWEEN TWO OPPOSITE VICES

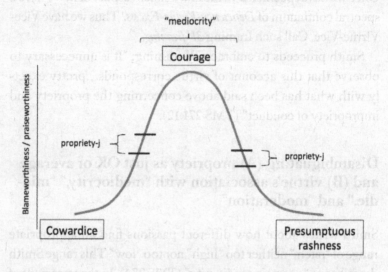

On the right-hand slope of the hill we have *another* propriety band, now separating courage (praiseworthy) from presumptuous rashness (blameworthy). Using two proprieties, then, we have a "mediocrity" within which lies praiseworthy behavior.

Funny as it sounds, at the middle of this mediocrity lies peak praiseworthiness.

Only a few of the sentences in TMS strike me as regrettable, but here I treat one of them. In the following block quotation, the regrettable sentence is the last one, which I have put in italics:

> The propriety of every passion excited by objects peculiarly related to ourselves, the pitch which the spectator can go along with, must lie, it is evident, in a certain mediocrity. If the passion is too high, or if it is too low, he cannot enter into it. Grief and resentment for private misfortunes and injuries may easily, for example, be too high,

PROPRIETY IN ADAM SMITH 15

and in the greater part of mankind they are so. ... *This mediocrity, however, in which the point of propriety consists, is different in different passions.* (TMS 27.1-2, italics added)

If I could travel back in time and suggest edits to Smith, I would propose that he replace the italicized sentence with the following: "This mediocrity, however, which is bound on every side by a point of propriety, is different for different passions."

Smith also speaks of virtue as a sort of *moderation*: "Considered as the quality of an action, it [virtue] consists, even according to Aristotle, in the reasonable moderation of the affection from which the action proceeds" (TMS 271.13). The idea of moderation should be understood as there being a primary passion which needs to be checked, and that checking is done by *another passion*. Virtue then entails moderation between these two passions.

Understanding that the checking force is also a passion helps us to understand, too, that any 3V-framing is flippable, just as "right" and "left" flip when we turn the map upside-down: We can frame deficiency/excess either in terms of the primary or the checking passion.

Propriety in a single aspect and overall

Figure 2.2 offers a two-sided depiction of the virtuousness of an action. But an action or piece of conduct may have several important aspects—aspects aside from courage—and the deficiency-excess framing may be applied to each aspect. Now let's move from two-sided moderation to N-sided moderation, balancing various salient or pertinent aspects.

It seems to me that, in judging conduct, the propriety-as-just-OK idea needs to be deployed in two different ways: first, in judging the action in regard to a single aspect (or a single set of aspects), and second, in judging the action overall (or, over all pertinent aspects). Here, Smith is not explicit about the distinction, nor about whether he is employing both ways of judging conduct. But both ways are found in TMS, and I think it fair to say that he employs both.

To illustrate, let me offer an analogy of Bill Mazeroski, a baseball player who in fielding (defense) far surpassed standard levels, but in hitting (offense) was perhaps only a little above the standard (he batted .260 lifetime). So, in fielding, Mazeroski was super-duper. But as a baseball player *overall* he was perhaps only great. (He was inducted into the Hall of Fame in 2001, 29 years after his retirement.) Here we see the contrast between evaluation in regard to a single aspect and evaluation overall.

But the single aspect vs. overall contrast is itself something that can be zoomed in and zoomed out: We might zoom in and confine the conversation to fielding alone, and speak of overall fielding ability, then break that down into aspects of fielding (catching, range, throwing, etc.). Or we might zoom out to a larger game of human life, and say that Mazeroski was great in the single aspect of playing baseball, then inquire after his quality as a human being overall.

When it comes to the virtues treated by Smith, we can see the same distinction between single-aspect and overall virtue. What Smith writes for the virtues could also be applied to baseball skills: "[W]ho is so perfect as not to have many superiors in many different qualifications?" (TMS 248.25).

In TMS we find the following passage, in which Smith explicitly associates propriety with suitableness "to all the circumstances"—that is, overall suitableness—as opposed to any single aspect:

> The propriety of a person's behaviour, depends not upon
> its suitableness to any one circumstance of his situation,

but to all the circumstances, which, when we bring his
case home to ourselves, we feel, should naturally call
upon his attention. If he appears to be so much occupied
by any one of them, as entirely to neglect the rest, we
disapprove of his conduct, as something which we cannot entirely go along with, because not properly adjusted
to all the circumstances of his situation.... (TMS 202.5)

Smith provides an illustration: "A parent in private life might, upon
the loss of an only son, express without blame a degree of grief and
tenderness, which would be unpardonable in a general at the head
of an army, when glory, and the public safety, demanded so great
a part of his attention" (TMS 202.5).

Smith speaks of "all the circumstances" and I speak of "overall," but overall judgments do not really consider all conceivable
aspects, because aspects are innumerable. When we come to overall judgments, what we do, of course, is consider the aspects that
strike us as the most important, that "call upon" our attention. We
give less thought to other, seemingly less important aspects.

Smith associates overall evaluation with the term *propriety*. But
the passage comes in Part V, and I do not read it as reserving the
term *propriety* for overall evaluation, but as clarifying that the term
also applies, or even most importantly applies, to overall evaluation.
Early in TMS, Smith develops a way of evaluating action in regard
to a single aspect, and there, too, uses the term *propriety*.

Seeing the propriety-as-just-OK idea as applying both to the
judging of behavior in single aspects and to judging it overall is natural. The contrast between single aspects and overall judgment is
also natural. Whenever an overall judgment is questioned or debated, "we generally cast about for other arguments" (TMS 89.8), or
particular aspects, that help us come to an overall judgment or

to defend the overall judgment that we assume (see TMS 189.7). As we saw, Mazeroski's overall fielding grade is only an aspect of his overall ballplayer grade, which is but an aspect of his overall human-being grade.

Propriety ladders

Propriety depends on a particular community or reference group. I think it is appropriate on our part to read into Smith an idea of a sequence of communities ordered by rising standards.

A ladder has a sequence of rungs. In the real world a ladder has a lowest rung and a highest rung, which makes the ladder analogy misleading. But if we think of a ladder with neither a clearly defined lowermost rung nor a clearly defined uppermost rung, I think we may profitably speak of a "propriety ladder."

The idea of a propriety ladder does not find clear expression in Smith's writings, but it is there, if only implicitly. It is implied by two features of Smith's thought. First, the stepping from one level to a higher level, from community j to community j+1. Once we recognize stepping from j to j+1, we simply iterate the idea and step from j+1 to j+2, and so on. The second key feature of Smith's thought is that he formulates moral concepts in a way that discourages thinking in terms of a lowermost or an uppermost. Such open-endedness ensures that the iteration just spoken of is possible, and, thus, we have a ladder that, at either end, has not a terminal rung but an ellipsis.

Smith distinguishes one level of propriety from another when he explains that the admiration we feel for great actions arises from our perception of "the great, the noble, and exalted propriety of such actions" (TMS 192.11). To speak of a propriety that is great, noble, and exalted is to perceive a propriety above ordinary propriety. Elsewhere, Smith contrasts a self-restraint that arises from a "vulgar prudence" and a self-restraint that arises from "the sense of propriety," and says the former constitutes "a propriety and virtue of a much inferior order" to the latter (TMS 263.5).

Likewise, Smith speaks of a "superior prudence," which is a prudence "combined with many greater and more splendid virtues, with valour, with extensive and strong benevolence, with a sacred regard to the rules of justice, and all these supported by a proper degree of self-command" (TMS 216.15). "This superior prudence," Smith says, "when carried to the highest degree of perfection, necessarily supposes the art, the talent, and the habit or disposition of acting with the most perfect propriety in every possible circumstance and situation" (ibid).[2] Thus, Smith ascends the ladder to where we find "the most perfect propriety." "None but those of the happiest mould are capable of suiting, with exact justness, their sentiments and behaviour to the smallest difference of situation, and of acting upon all occasions with the most delicate and accurate propriety" (TMS 162.1).

The exaltedness of the most accurate propriety may be visualized as a fine range of "mediocrity" in Figure 2.2: Imagine two propriety lines narrowly straddling the peak of the curve. In difficult situations, this is the idea of complete perfection, which "no human conduct ever did, or ever can come up to" (TMS 26.9).

Sports prowess again provides an analogy. We see rising standards in the various levels or leagues of a sport. But sports also serve as a foil, for there is something that we see quite clearly in sports that we do not see nearly as clearly in the moral arena. In sports, there is close agreement about quality. In tennis, the match itself is

---

2. On perfection as the first standard, see TMS 25-6.7–9, 247–249.23–26; on "particular instances" that guide us, see 187–88.2 and 159.8; on wonder, admiration, and emulation see 20.3, 114.3, 335–336.23–24, 117.9, 75.3, 323.10, 192.11, 247.25.

governed by rules that are precise and accurate. The two contenders simply play each other and we see who wins. If plain spectatorship is insufficient, statistics and other metrics lead the experts to agree remarkably closely about who is best. Tennis experts might disagree a bit about who is better, but they can agree remarkably well on the ladder itself.

When it comes to the moral arena, however, the looseness and complexity of the rules mean that we should recognize disagreement and confusion not only over how best to formulate the rungs of a ladder (that is, whether we are talking community j or community j+1) but over whole ladders, whole sequences of proprieties. In considering hospitality, any two people will often find that they have differently formulated ladders—that is, they have different notions of what constitutes hospitality and what improvements in it look like.

Even if one person were to come to see how the other person formulates the hospitality "ladder," she may often disagree with its propriety. Yes, to judge the different formulations we return yet again, now at an even deeper level, to...a sense of propriety! Smith teaches us that such problems inhere in all of the becoming virtues, for example, courage, friendship, generosity, temperance—even gratitude and prudence.

Tennis has pretty clear, determinate standards of excellence, and highly visible top performers. Morality has neither.

Concluding remark

If your head is spinning, I hope it's in a good way. When we don't know where we are, sometimes we feel lost. But other times we enjoy the adventure.

Smith well knew that propriety involves unending spirals and indeterminacies. People are bound to disagree on propriety. Could it be that that is a chief lesson of TMS? Could that be why Smith emphasizes commutative justice and its specialness? Even amidst the wildest blooming confusion, commutative justice offers a social grammar both for the enjoyment of personal tranquility and for flourishing adventures in propriety.

CHAPTER 3

A Better Understanding of Justice

Today's call for "social justice" offers an unhelpful explanation of what the concept of justice might entail. Adam Smith is a better guide.

"There is simply no such thing as 'social' justice," writes Jordan Peterson (at Twitter on November 16, 2021). "Whatever those who rely on this clichéd phrase are aiming at has nothing whatsoever to do with justice. Justice is meted out at the level of the suffering individual" (ibid). Indeed, if the term "social justice" rightly suggests a larger idea of justice beyond simply leaving others in peace, it offers an unhelpful explanation of what that larger idea might entail. Instead of seeking to divine the meaning of "social justice," a better course would be to consider Adam Smith's three-layered concept of justice.

In *The Theory of Moral Sentiments*, Smith distinguishes between commutative justice, or not messing with other people's stuff; distributive justice, or making a becoming use of what is one's own; and estimative justice, or estimating objects properly. When a claim not to have our possessions messed with is made against government, it is called liberty. Yet even classical liberals can sense that justice extends farther. What, after all, justifies commutative justice or liberty but some larger principles?

In expanding the concept of justice, it is natural to think that we should move on to some other sense of justice, such as "social justice" or "general justice." For Smith, however, justice is always a matter of individual actions and duties. If someone does something, the relevant questions are: Did he, in doing the action, mess with anyone's stuff? Did he make a becoming use of his own possessions? Did he estimate pertinent objects properly? The first is a matter of grammar-like rules. But the second and third, distributive and estimative, involve aesthetic considerations and a sense of propriety—above which is praiseworthy and below which is blameworthy.

Distributive and estimative justice necessarily involve vagueness, as in Smith's use of the word "becoming." Smith described their rules as "loose, vague, and indeterminate." Each sense of justice demands an evaluation of the actor and his action, in light of the context of that action and the relevant alternatives. Estimative justice demands specification of the object being estimated. Such demands give more structure, coherence, and discipline than is found in discourse about "social" or "general" justice.

Conflating distributive and estimative justice forsakes their distinct operations, and the result is sloppier thinking. Some contend that in estimating an object, one is distributing one's esteem, and such distributing is then judged for its becomingness. But this expansion does not work well. Where Smith explicitly writes of "distributive justice," it is associated with "proper beneficence," "charity or generosity," "the social virtues," "the social and beneficent Virtues," and giving praise that is due. It seems that the objects of distributive justice attach to a set of persons; distributive justice would not apply to a poem, a picture, or an idea abstracted from any particular set of persons.

Moreover, to say that we have a limited supply of esteem to distribute to all of the objects of the world usually works poorly. Such a metaphor would need some notion of the constraint on esteem, as well as some sense of the relevant objects over which such points are to be distributed. But, for estimative justice, we are talking about all manner of objects, including ideas. Ideas are innumerable. One idea soon gives rise to another.

Ideas and sentiments form concatenations, and a single alteration might render the concatenation deserving of a much different estimation. The alteration makes for a new and distinct concatenation. Distributive justice involves a sense of confronting a robust set of objects—people, particularly those "connected" to us—over which one is to distribute one's social resources. But with estimative justice, we do not have much sense of a complete set of objects.

Estimative justice is a more elementary operator than distributive; its elements do not of themselves make for distribution of a set of resources to another set of objects. The minimal nature of estimative justice, Smith says, makes it "still more extensive" than distributive justice. Estimative justice is naturally recursive. If one justice swallows another, it is estimative that swallows up both distributive and commutative. Estimative justice is like a whale that swallows up all objects presented to it.

There's another good reason to keep distributive and estimative justice distinct. The move that we applied to commutative justice, to create a claim, called a right or liberty, is a move that naturally accedes as well to distributive justice. Steve, a friend of Jim's, may justly talk of having a loose sort of claim on Jim's time or other resources, though not by promise or contract—that is, not by commutative justice. It attends, rather, distributive justice, and is only a loose or imperfect right.

For estimative justice, however, such a move is far messier: estimative justice is justice done to an object—such as a poem, a picture, or an idea—and it does not make much sense to say that a poem, a picture, or an idea enjoys a claim or a right.

Consider a public policy issue—say, the federal prohibition on payments for organs, such as kidneys. The prohibition is, first of all, a violation of commutative justice, in that it has the government messing with other people's stuff, by initiating coercion (including threat thereof) against non-coercers, notably would-be kidney transactors. Second, one's failing to oppose the prohibition would be estimatively unjust, in that it would be overestimating prohibition relative to the alternative (liberalization). We may also say that the advocate of prohibition is distributively unjust, in that he makes an unbecoming use of his own, in advocating prohibition.

It is important to embrace Smith's tri-layered justice. Respecting the logic of each layer helps us to see more clearly what we are talking about and where we agree and disagree. Such clarity will help to show where vagueness inheres, why it does, and just how sprawling and challenging that vagueness is. Thus, Smith's tri-layered understanding teaches us humility in advancing assertions about the loose, vague, and indeterminate facets. It teaches us to refrain from calling loudly, in matters beyond commutative justice.

Seeing the three layers of justice enables us to appreciate commutative justice. By distinguishing it cogently, we better see its crucial role in providing a social grammar. If you recognize the need to understand justice in a way that extends beyond commutative justice, you should engage with Smith. He guides us on how to talk justice beyond the commutative: formulate it as either distributive or estimative, not an admixture of the two.

CHAPTER 4

Adam Smith and Human Resources: The Moral Challenges of Modern Society

I n the times of Erasmus and Martin Luther and after, printing and literacy cracked interpretation wide open—interpretation of scripture, of politics, of work, of life, of life after death. Consciousness got a lot more complicated.

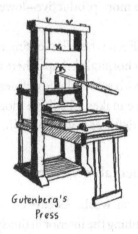

Gutenberg's Press

Man evolved for life in small cohesive bands, and our genes have not changed that much since the small band of 12,000 years ago. And then came social hierarchy. But traditional society worked to enforce social cohesion and to keep interpretation closed. Since Luther, however, many forces have tended otherwise, toward discohesion and moral confusion, busting interpretation open.

Some of our most influential thinkers, such as Jean-Jacques Rousseau, have accentuated discohesion. Others, including Adam Smith, treated it less than squarely. They did not want to raise alarm about how modern developments—in literacy, science, technology, commerce, jurisprudence, and politics—might tend to undo traditional

Gutenberg's Press. Source: Drawing by Dave Gray, https://www.flickr.com/photos/davegray/6319799633/sizes/m/in/photostream/.

forms of social cohesion.

But treating it less than squarely does not mean that Smith did not treat it profoundly. Here I highlight elements of Smith as they relate to moral challenges of modern society, especially in work and employment. Smith inspires the individual to make a place for himself in society, a useful and satisfying place, by contributing.

Competence is key, but the crucial competence is *in sympathy*. The individual needs competence in sympathy to find a place to work and contribute and to find his own life satisfying. As moral counselor, Smith helps the worker and the employer.

By "sympathy" Smith meant fellow feeling or shared sentiment. Deftness in sympathizing might be thought of as social intelligence. It's crucial to the social virtues. Sympathetic deftness is a kind of competence or ability. Employers are wise to look for it. Workers with sympathetic deftness are more productive—lower cost, higher revenue.

And there is a pleasure in sympathy. Even when the sentiment that is shared is an unpleasant one, as at a hospital perhaps, there is a pleasure in the sharing of it. Workers with sympathetic deftness are nicer to be around. A nice workplace makes jobs there more attractive to *other* workers. Sympathetic deftness is win-win-win.

The amiable virtues and the respectable virtues

Take the situation of Jim working in a car wash. As cars come through the line he's having trouble vacuuming the interior in timely fashion. A coworker, Mary, needs to coordinate her activities with his. There are two sides of sympathy. In order to help Jim improve his performance, Mary must *enter into* Jim's situation, because she needs to simulate his experience, in her imagination, to discover the sentiments of someone in his situation. Smith speaks of "the soft, the gentle, the amiable virtues," shown here by Mary (TMS 23.1).

But if Jim seeks help from Mary, he must meet her halfway. He cannot grieve and moan. He must buck up. Smith speaks of the "respectable" virtues, the virtues of "self-command" and "self-government," shown here by Jim (TMS 23.1, 25.6, and 237ff).

To find sympathy, then, Mary needs to exercise the amiable virtues, and Jim the respectable. In that way they can find enough fellow feeling to work an improvement: Perhaps Mary shows Jim how to vacuum more quickly or adjusts the process or joins Jim in an appeal for better equipment or someone to assist Jim.

My choice of names, "Mary" and "Jim," to illustrate the amiable and respectable virtues coincide with some gendering in Smith's work. Smith suggests that the amiable virtues come more naturally to women, the respectable to men, if only in terms of comparative advantages (TMS 151.32, 187.1, 190.10, 209.13; LRBL 131, 192).

But the upward path of virtue calls for both. We need to be amiable to become more respectable, and respectable to become more amiable. The path winds in an upward spiral.

If Jim is to buck up so as to help Mary to be able to enter into his situation, he must understand *her* situation, which is the amiable one of entering into his. And if Mary is to enter into Jim's situation, she must imagine what it's like *for him to buck up*, so she must understand the respectable virtues to exercise the amiable

ones. "The man who feels the most for the joys and sorrows of others, is best fitted for acquiring the most complete control of his own joys and sorrows" (TMS 152.36). The interrelation between amiable and respectable is one of many yin-yangs in Smith's moral theory.

https://en.wikipedia.org/wiki/Yin_and_yang#/media/File:Yin_yang.svg

Habitual sympathy in the workplace

In a workplace, resources and activities are combined or concatenated to produce results. That concatenation of resources involves innumerable points of mutual coordination between workers like Jim and Mary. Jim and Mary need sympathy to mutually coordinate their actions to improve the overall coordination of the concatenation. The word for such mutual efforts is *cooperation*. Jim and Mary need sympathy *to cooperate* in the workplace. Think of that verb as *co-operate*, like the verb *cowrite* as in "Lennon and McCartney cowrote many songs." Jim and Mary are two of many co-operators in the overall concatenation of resources and activities, and they work together, by moments of sympathy, to co-operate the workings of their workplace.

Coworkers Jim and Mary would come to know each other's charms and quirks and form a habit of sympathizing with one another: "What is called affection, is in reality nothing but habitual sympathy" (TMS 220.7). We speak of affection toward friends and family, but it also arises among familiars in the workplace. When relations are "placed in situations which naturally create this habitual sympathy…[w]e generally find that it actually does take place; we therefore naturally expect that it should; and we are, upon that account, more shocked when, upon any occasion, we find that it does not" (TMS 220.7). A coworker becomes a *workmate*. You should get along with your coworkers; you should become workmates.

Smith speaks of habitual sympathy among colleagues:

> Colleagues in office, partners in trade, call one another
> brothers; and frequently feel towards one another as if
> they really were so. Their good agreement is an advan-

tage to all; and, if they are tolerably reasonable people, they are naturally disposed to agree. We expect that they should do so; and their disagreement is a sort of small scandal. The Romans expressed this sort of attachment by the word *necessitudo*, which, from the etymology, seems to denote that it was imposed by the necessity of the situation. (TMS 224.15)

There may be things about your workmates that rankle, but *necessitudo* is part of the job. It calls on you to get along. It calls for sympathetic deftness.

In sympathy you and your workmates learn to smooth over the things that rankle. Maybe you do things that rankle your workmates and need to adjust. The adjustment process calls for sympathy, which calls for virtues amiable and respectable. Maybe you need to buck up—that is, you need to *command* quirky passions which rankle your workmates. By sympathy you learn to improve your conduct.

Reputation

In sympathy you realize how others perceive you—and what they may tell others about you. Sympathetic deftness isn't only a social virtue. It's the better part of prudence. If you rankle people, they might damage your reputation. If you delight your workmates, they will enhance it. Reputation is other people's estimations, as expressed in their words, of your merit and trustworthiness.

Reputation starts locally but extends farther. Think how far your credit record extends, when communicated to potential employers, creditors, and landlords by Experian, TransUnion, or Equifax.

Reputation is a glue of the modern world. Smith said that a

merchant "is afraid of losing his character, and is scrupulous in observing every engagement" (LJ 538). He explained the incentives:

> When a person makes perhaps 20 contracts in a day, he cannot gain so much by endeavoring to impose on his neighbors, as the very appearance of a cheat would make him lose.... Wherever dealings are frequent, a man does not expect to gain so much by any one contract as by probity and punctuality in the whole, and a prudent dealer, who is sensible of his real interest, would rather choose to lose what he has a right to than give any ground for suspicion. (LJ 538–9)

And Smith said that in modern society, we all are merchants: "Every man thus lives by exchanging, or becomes in some measure a merchant, and the society itself grows to be what is properly a commercial society" (WN 37.1). We all live by reputation. Our immersion in work and trade makes us honest and trustworthy even with strangers: "When the greater part of people are merchants they always bring probity and punctuality into fashion, and these therefore are the principal virtues of a commercial nation" (LJ 539).

"The real and effectual discipline which is exercised over a workman," Smith said, is not so much regulatory requirements, but his acceptance by his employers: "It is the fear of losing...employment which restrains his frauds and corrects his negligence" (WN 146.31).

If reputation is a glue to markets, sympathy is a glue to reputation—the glue behind the glue. Reputation is gossip about sympathetic experiences, and the communication of reputation is another scene of sympathy.

Character

Jim's virtues are exhibited in his conduct. In working with Jim, Mary sees his conduct and discerns patterns of conduct; she begins to see what motivates Jim, what constitutes his purposes, what he finds meaningful, and what he is after. She forms a sense of Jim's *character*. Jim's conduct is a reflection of his character. Mary's sympathetic deftness helps her to learn Jim's character.

Employers are interested in learning the character of an employee. What motivates Jim? Is he trustworthy? Does he strive to improve his abilities? Does he show concern for coworkers and customers? Does he understand *necessitudo*, the need to get on with coworkers?

Employers and coworkers use sympathetic imagination to get a sense of something deep and obscure about Jim. The question of Jim's character relates to that of his *conscience*.

The man within the breast

In treating the conscience, Smith developed a metaphor: the man within the breast. Jim's conscience is like a man within Jim's breast, continually monitoring Jim's conduct and calling Jim out when he can't go along with Jim's sentiments. When Jim acts in a way that is objectionable to the man within, the man within finds a sentiment that differs from the sentiment that motivated Jim's action. The difference constitutes *disapproval*. If the conscience is strong and if Jim is responsive, Jim suffers that disapproval; he comes to regret his action, to feel remorse; and he may learn to correct his habits and improve his conduct.

Jim's conscience is the source of the most important sort of reputation: the reputation he enjoys with his own man within the breast —his self-estimation.

The man within the breast, Smith says, is a representative of a being who either is merely like God in at least some respects or simply is God Himself (TMS 215.11). Whichever way that being is understood, the man within the breast is *a representative of* that being. Smith uses "impartial spectator" to signify various kinds of spectators, but one is a benevolent being of super knowledge and supreme moral judgment, like God. Although Smith says that the man within the breast, or conscience, is a representative of such impartial spectator, he makes clear that the man within the breast is *not necessarily a good representative* of the impartial spectator (see ch. 20). Our chief job in life is to make a better representative. Smith encourages us to improve the man within the breast.

The man within the breast approves of Jim when he shares the sentiments that Jim had in taking the action. Jim wants such approval, the pleasure of the sympathy of the man within the breast. Again, there is a pleasure in shared sentiment.

Thus, Smith turns sympathy *inward*: Jim's sympathy with himself. By reflecting now on his own conduct of yesterday, Jim of right now sees whether he can sympathize with Jim of yesterday. Smith writes: "I divide myself, as it were, into two persons;…I, the examiner and judge, represent a different character from that other I, the person whose conduct is examined into and judged of" (TMS 113.6).

When we reflect on our conduct of yesterday, we must be prepared to tell ourselves: "Yeah, I was kind of a jerk." Smith tells us that it is unpleasant to disapprove of our past conduct (TMS 158.4), but doing so is part of the respectable virtues: Admit that you can be a jerk. Admit it! Buck up! Respectable virtues work to improve our workplace conduct. Respectable virtues work to improve our amiable virtues.

Those we live with

Jim asks himself: "Was I a jerk to Mary yesterday?" Maybe he's not sure. Maybe Mary was a jerk and deserved the sharp words.

Smith writes:

> In solitude, we are apt to feel too strongly whatever relates to ourselves: we are apt to overrate the good offices we may have done, and the injuries we may have suffered…. The conversation of a friend brings us to a better, that of a stranger to a still better temper. The man within the breast…requires often to be awakened and put in mind of his duty, by the presence of the real spectator. (TMS 153.38)

Still unsure about whether he had been a jerk, Jim may seek some counsel. Smith would tell Jim: Talk to those you live with. Share your experience with a friend or family member—a familiar who shows the amiable virtues toward you. Report the matter candidly, thinking, "I know I can be a jerk." Let the friend imagine the situation and discover her own sentiment in the simulated situation. If her sentiment corresponds with yours, she will tend to approve of your conduct. And if not, to disapprove. Listen to your friend.

Friends and family are counselors. They have habits of sympathizing with us: They feel affection for us. They know us better than others do. They know our character, what we're "about." We depend on our friends.

Counsel is part of friendship, but its soul is affection. More important than fame, wealth, or glory is the "confidence, the esteem, and love of those we live with" (TMS 166.8). They are the ones who know us best (see Clark and Lee 2017).

The problem of partiality

We develop and maintain friendships with people who tend to take our side. The problem with the counsel of friends is the pleasure of shared sentiment and the unpleasantness of disapproval. We like people like us. Those who are most kind to us are those of our own kind. Our friends are *partial* toward us (Forman-Barzilai 2010).

A certain partiality is, no doubt, part of friendship, but nonetheless friends are often too partial. It is good that they enter into our situation, but it is *not good* if they neglect the situation of the other party to a dispute. They don't get to hear her side of the story.

Notice in the block quotation above that Smith said that the conversation *of a stranger* brings us to an even better temper. Smith writes: "We can venture to express more emotion in the presence of a friend than in that of a stranger, because we expect more indulgence from the one than from the other" (TMS 207.10).

So even the feedback of our friends needs review. Once again things come back to the man within the breast, the conscience.

The bustle and business of the world

The conscience is a work in progress; it is a job that lasts the days of our life. Life should be balanced with hours of cool reflection or sympathy with the man within the breast; hours of sympathy with friends and family; and, finally, hours of sympathy with others: strangers, trading partners, shop clerks, coworkers, people of the world—*unfamiliars*. We need to sympathize with unfamiliars as well as familiars.

Smith tells us that virtue develops over the lifetime. The development brings forth, we hope, the "just man who has been thoroughly bred in the great school of self-command, in **the bustle and business of the world**" (TMS 146.25, emphasis added).

Bustle and business draw us into moments of sympathy with unfamiliars. Although brief and shallow, those moments of sympathy put us in mind of someone who has no special partiality toward us. The world's bustle and business teach us to see ourselves at a distance, as but a small part of a greater whole. As we realize our dependence on the institutions and market relations of that greater whole, we learn to care for its well-being, and to ponder how our own small part contributes to such well-being. To help us appreciate our part in the worldwide economy, Smith wrote *The Wealth of Nations*.

Sympathy in modern society

Smith saw human beings as creatures who yearn for sentiment that is shared by all, that encompasses "we, the people"; it is as though Smith knew that we had evolved from small hunter-gatherer bands.

The dream is a utopia "[w]here the necessary assistance is reciprocally afforded from love, from gratitude, from friendship, and esteem…. All the different members of [society] are bound together by the agreeable bands of love and affection, and are, as it were, drawn to one common centre of mutual good offices" (TMS 85.1).

But modern society has no "common centre of mutual good offices," and it is horribly misguided to aim to recreate the encompassing sentiment of the small, closed, simple society. The modern world is here, a morally confusing society, with interpretation busted wide open. And there is no going back.

We have seen some of Smith's teaching about how to cope in the modern world. We have seen three seats of sympathy:

1. Sympathy with familiars, those we live with.

2. Sympathy with unfamiliars, which calls forth common decency and civility.

3.   Sympathy with the man within the breast, or *soul sympathy*.

Notice how in the small, closed, simple society—like the ancestral band that produced our genes—the first and third would coincide (with no place for unfamiliars). But that is no longer the world we live in. We have to get used to that, and Smith helps us.

The three seats of sympathy—familiars, unfamiliars, and the soul—are crucial to one's well-being in modern society. They won't recreate the strong social cohesion of the small band, but they are what we have to work with. All three call for sympathetic deftness. By improving the amiable and respectable virtues we can enhance our reputation with employers, customers, and trading partners. We can enhance affection among friends, family, and workmates. And we can secure greater tranquility within our own breast.

CHAPTER 5

Grateful to Whom, or What?

My dear George Mason Economics colleague Donald
Boudreaux (2019) looks back "with enormous gratitude" on his 61 years of life. The expression, he says,
"isn't about his parents." He expresses his gratitude for the blessing
of the modern world. Bryan Caplan (Caplan 2017), another dear
colleague, expresses his gratitude similarly. And Jonah Goldberg,
in his great book *Suicide of the West*, writes of the gratitude we all
should feel for what he calls "the Miracle" of liberal civilization
(Goldberg 2018).

Caplan and Goldberg say what they are grateful *for*, but not
whom or what they are grateful *to*. But Boudreaux does: "Thank
you, modernity. Thank you, market-tested innovation. Thank you,
private property and the rule of law."

Their welcome sentiments offer an occasion to explore the spirit.
Adam Smith writes: "[B]efore any thing can be the proper object
of gratitude or resentment, it must not only be the cause of pleasure
or pain; it must likewise be capable of feeling them" (TMS 94.3).

Let us suppose that Jim feels gratitude to his benefactor Bob.
Smith says that "before any thing [such as Bob]...can be the complete and proper object" of gratitude, "it must be the cause of pleasure," "it must be capable of feeling those sensations," and "it must
not only have produced those sensations, but it must have produced them from design, and from a design that is approved of"
(TMS 96.6).

Smith goes further: "What gratitude chiefly desires, is not only to make the benefactor [Bob] feel pleasure in his turn, but to make him conscious that he meets with this reward on account of his past conduct, to make him pleased with that conduct, and to satisfy him that the person [Jim] upon whom he bestowed his good offices was not unworthy of them" (TMS 95.4).

Query set 1: Is gratitude-*to* an inherent facet of gratitude? That is, can gratitude exist as gratitude for something without being gratitude to someone or something? If it can, should we call it gratefulness (rather than gratitude)? On the other hand, if gratitude-*to* is an inherent facet of gratitude, then to whom or what are Caplan and Goldberg grateful?

Query set 2: Boudreaux expresses gratitude to modernity, market-tested innovation, private property, and the rule of law. Do those things work in the Smith passages above? Can they enter into Boudreaux's joys and comforts, and reflect on his feeling of gratitude? Do they act with a design to aid Boudreaux?

Query set 3: Perhaps one would say that Boudreaux, Caplan, and Goldberg speak in a summary way of the many individuals whose actions have brought forth the blessings they enjoy. It is to those myriad individuals that they are grateful. If so, does it matter that those individuals don't in fact know anything of their enjoyments, nor their gratitude, had multifarious designs, and in fact may now be deceased? If Bob is deceased or unidentified, how is Jim "to make him conscious that he meets with this reward on account of his past conduct" etc.?

Just prior to the passages quoted above, Smith writes:

> We conceive ... a sort of gratitude for those inanimat-
> ed objects which have been the causes of great or fre-
> quent pleasure to us. The sailor, who, as soon as he got
> ashore, should mend his fire with the plank upon which
> he had just escaped from a shipwreck, would seem to
> be guilty of an unnatural action. We should expect that
> he would rather preserve it with care and affection, as
> a monument that was, in some measure, dear to him....
> The house which we have long lived in, the tree whose
> verdure and shade we have long enjoyed, are both looked
> upon with a sort of respect that seems due to such bene-
> factors. The decay of the one, or the ruin of the other,
> affects us with a kind of melancholy, though we should
> sustain no loss by it. The Dryads and the Lares of the
> ancients, a sort of genii of trees and houses, were prob-
> ably first suggested by this sort of affection which the
> authors of those superstitions felt for such objects, and
> which seemed unreasonable, if there was nothing ani-
> mated about them. (TMS 94.2)

Similarly, in the *History of Astronomy*, Smith writes:

> The reverence and gratitude, with which some of the
> appearances of nature inspire him, convince him that
> they are the proper objects of reverence and gratitude,
> and therefore proceed from some intelligent beings, who
> take pleasure in the expressions of those sentiments.
> With him, therefore, every object of nature, which by its
> beauty or greatness, its utility or hurtfulness, is consid-

erable enough to attract his attention, and whose operations are not perfectly regular, is supposed to act by the
direction of some invisible and designing power.... The
tree which now flourishes and now decays, is inhabited
by a Dryad, upon whose health or sickness its various
appearances depend. (EPS, 49)

Query 4: How neatly does what Smith says about a
"complete and proper object" of gratitude fit gratitude
to God?

Smith writes: "Gratitude and resentment...are in every respect,
it is evident, counterparts to one another" (TMS, 76.7). He writes:

We are angry, for a moment, even at the stone that hurts
us. A child beats it, a dog barks at it, a choleric man is apt
to curse it. The least reflection, indeed, corrects this sentiment, and we soon become sensible, that what has no
feeling is a very improper object of revenge. When the
mischief, however, is very great, the object which caused
it becomes disagreeable to us ever after, and we take
pleasure to burn or destroy it. We should treat, in this
manner, the instrument which had accidentally been the
cause of the death of a friend, and we should often think
ourselves guilty of a sort of inhumanity, if we neglected
to vent this absurd sort of vengeance upon it. (TMS, 94.1)

Friedrich Hayek used "resent" in criticizing "social justice" and
in advancing the atavism thesis about modern collectivist politics.
He wrote:

Their demand for a just distribution in which organized power is to be used to allocate to each what he deserves, is thus strictly an *atavism*, based on primordial emotions. (Hayek 1979, 165)

But these habits had to be shed again to make the transition to the market economy and the open society possible. The steps of this transition were all breaches of that 'solidarity' which governed the small group and which are still resented. (Hayek 1979, 162)

It was this unavoidable attenuation of the content of our obligations, which necessarily accompanied their extension, that people with strongly ingrained moral emotions resented. (Hayek 1978, 66)

Hayek (1976, 67) said that "social justice" is "an attempt to satisfy a craving inherited from the traditions of the small group but which is meaningless in the Great Society of free men". Hayek (1988, 140) suggested that "perhaps most people can conceive of abstract tradition only as a personal Will." He then asked: "If so, will they not be inclined to find this will in 'society' in an age in which more overt supernaturalisms are ruled out as superstitions?"

Query set 5: If the resentment that some people feel toward liberal institutions ("capitalism") is superstitious and atavistic, would we say the same for the gratitude of Boudreaux, Caplan, and Goldberg? If not, why not?

CHAPTER 6

The Regularity of Irregularity in Adam Smith's Three Invisible Hands

Smith strikes that perfect equipoise between irony and encomium which is so typical of him.

– Knud Haakonssen (1981, 91)

Only an irregular event, such as a lightning storm, Adam Smith said, would have prompted the "savages" of "Heathen antiquity" to invoke as explanation "the invisible hand of Jupiter." Smith told of "that vulgar superstition which ascribes all the irregular events of nature to the favour or displeasure of intelligent, though invisible beings, to gods, daemons, witches, genii, fairies" (EPS, 49). "[I]t is the irregular events of nature only that are ascribed to the agency and power of their gods" (ibid). "Their ignorance, and confusion of thought, necessarily gave birth to that pusillanimous superstition, which ascribes almost every unexpected event, to the arbitrary will of some designing, though invisible beings" (EPS 112). Earlier, in 1709, John Trenchard had elaborated the idea in *The Natural History of Superstition* (Trenchard 1709). William Grampp (2000) said, "the invisible hand has a pejorative connotation in the *Essay on Astronomy*" (448).

But in TMS and WN, Smith uses "invisible hand" in the course of explaining certain *regularities* in social affairs. Alec Macfie treated the matter in a well-known article, saying "the *capricious* role of 'the invisible hand of Jupiter' is quite different from that of the order-preserving 'invisible hand' in the two books" (Macfie 1971, 197). Scholars have sometimes endorsed the idea that Jupiter pertains to a sense of irregularity while the two others to regularity.[1]

There may, however, be subtlety in Smith's handiwork. Maybe a sense of irregularity inspired not only the "savage" to invoke an invisible hand, but likewise the author of TMS and WN. Despite the surface regularity, maybe irregularity lurks beneath in TMS and WN.

Smith's philosophy of science suggests a diachronic movement from irregularity to regularity. We no longer regard a lightning storm as dependent on Jupiter's mood. It's all part of a quite regular system of weather. We just had to enlarge the frame of observation and develop our interpretations. We pass from irregularity to regularity.

Smith writes:

> Nature...seems to abound with events which appear solitary and incoherent with all that go before them, which therefore disturb the easy movement of the imagination; which makes its ideas succeed each other, if one may say so, by irregular starts and sallies.... Philosophy, by representing the invisible chains which bind together all these disjointed objects, endeavours to introduce order into this chaos of jarring and discordant appearances, to allay this tumult of the imagination, and to restore it, when it surveys the great revolutions of the universe, to

1. E.g., Aydinonat (2008, 80); C. Smith (2006, 12–13, 82); see also Kennedy (2009, 378–9).

that tone of tranquillity and composure, which is both
most agreeable in itself, and most suitable to its nature.
(EPS 45–6)

Philosophy thus restores us to a sense of regularity. Once we
have enlarged our thinking, "custom and the frequent repetition
of any object comes at last to form and bend the mind or organ to
that habitual mood and disposition which fits them to receive its
impression, without undergoing any very violent change" (EPS 37).

David Hume had likewise associated irregularity with a naïve
invocation of invisible agency: "It is only on the discovery of extraor-
dinary phaenomena, such as earthquakes, pestilence, and prodigies
of any kind, that [the generality of mankind] find themselves at a
loss to assign a proper cause.... It is usual for men, in such difficulties, to have recourse to some invisible intelligent principle as the
immediate cause of that event which surprises them" (2000, 55).

But, for Hume, naïvete is perennial: "[P]hilosophers, who carry
their scrutiny a little farther, immediately perceive that, even in the
most familiar events, the energy of the cause is as unintelligible as
in the most unusual, and that we only learn by experience the frequent Conjunction of objects, without being ever able to compre-
hend anything like Connexion between them" (55). Start with any
ordinary object and ask why it exists. You provide an explanation.
With an enlargement of mind come new formulations, and new
objects for contemplation. Turn your explanation into an object to
be explained—*Why?*, *why?*, *why?*, without end. Think of it as explanation raised to the *i*th power, with *i* unbounded upward. By its
nature the process is unfinishable. Like Hume, Smith noted that
beyond the layers of explanation we have mystery, which "no philosopher has yet attempted to explain to us" (EPS, 146, 148). But
we get accustomed to that outer boundary.

Within that boundary, an irregularity prompts surprise and wonder, leading to enlargement and admiration but also the formulation of a new mysterious object, which may then, as we move into the next loop of the spiral, lead to the sense of irregularity, either from aberrations that confound us or from the question of causation at the next level, prompting again a sense of surprise and wonder, and so on. Smith admired the ongoing process, calling philosophy "the most sublime of all the agreeable arts" (EPS46).

Just as we see no irregularity in a lightning storm, the enlargement of philosophy may foster an enlarged sense of regularity in the whole. We much admire how all the parts are wonderfully adjusted to proper ends. William Paley (1802, 1) suggested that if, "in crossing a heath," we happen upon a watch, we should certainly infer a watchmaker. Smith had suggested something similar about the wonderful system of the universe:

> As soon as the Universe was regarded as a complete machine, as a coherent system, governed by general laws, and directed to general ends, viz. its own preservation and prosperity, and that of all the species that are in it; the resemblance which it evidently bore to the machines which are produced by human art, necessarily impressed those sages with a belief, that in the original formation of the world there must have been employed an art resembling the human art, but as much superior to it, as the world is superior to the machines which that art produces. (EPS 113–114)

Philosophy and science helped humankind along from polytheism to proper monotheism, Smith suggests: "as ignorance begot superstition, science gave birth to the first theism that arose among those nations, who were not enlightened by divine Revelation" (EPS 114). "As, in the rude ages of the world, whatever particular part of Nature excited the admiration of mankind, was apprehended to be animated by some particular divinity; so **the whole of Nature**, having, by [the Stoics'] reasonings, become equally the object of admiration, was equally apprehended to be animated by a Universal Deity" (EPS 116, emphasis added). In WN, Smith wrote of "that pure and rational religion, free from every mixture of absurdity, imposture, or fanaticism, such as wise men have **in all ages of the world** wished to see established" (WN 793.8, emphasis added).

Indeed, irrespective of how beautifully adjusted we feel its parts to be, we still may ask with Derek Parfit (1998): "[W]hy is there a Universe at all? It might have been true that nothing ever existed: no living beings, no stars, no atoms, not even space or time. When we think about this possibility, it can seem astonishing that anything exists." Parfit writes further: "I am reminded here of the aesthetic category of the sublime, as applied to the highest mountains, raging oceans, the night sky, the interiors of some cathedrals, and other things that are superhuman, awesome, limitless. No question is more sublime than why there is a Universe: why there is anything rather than nothing."

In *An Essay on the Sublime* published in 1747, John Baillie wrote: "it is in the *Almighty* that this Sublime is compleated, who with a *Nod* can shatter to Pieces the *Foundations* of a *Universe*, as with a *Word* he called it into *Being*" (1747, 21).

Let us use Paley's thought experiment as an analogy: In crossing the heath we happen upon—the universe.

If, in crossing the heath, it is the universe that we happen upon, the important question then is: What is the analogue of "crossing the heath"? Heaths that we know presuppose the universe that we know, so we must find an analogue to the heath to make any sense of happening upon the universe. That's no plain matter. After all, the very sense of our own existence would seem to presuppose the universe. But one way to put it might be an analogue of *utter nothingness*—the nonexistence of everything that we believe to exist.

And, as the saying goes, *ex nihilo nihil fit*—nothing comes from nothing. Utter nothingness would be the greatest regularity of all. Nothing comes from nothing—although, I suppose, it would, paradoxically, be a regularity that no one was around to experience.

In this respect, then, existence of the universe—including its laws, its creatures, and all regularities noted in their social affairs, including regularities of the free enterprise system—the whole shebang would itself be a great *irregularity* to the regularity of nothingness.

It is here that we might say that there is irregularity lurking behind Smith's two statements about people being "led by an invisible hand to...":

> They are **led by an invisible hand to** make nearly the same distribution of the necessaries of life, which would have been made, had the earth been divided into equal portions among all its inhabitants, and thus without intending it, without knowing it, advance the interest of the society, and afford means to the multiplication of the species. (TMS 184–5, emphasis added)

> By preferring the support of domestic to that of foreign industry, he intends only his own security; and by directing that industry in such a manner as its produce may be of the greatest value, he intends only his own gain, and he is in this, as in many other cases, **led by an invisible hand to** promote an end which was no part of his intention. (WN 456.9, italics added)

The "invisible hand" remarks belong to expositions of beneficial regularities in social processes, but they can be read—and are often read—as theistic affirmations about final causes (Oslington 2012; Harrison 2011, 47). As Macfie says: "The 'invisible hand of Jupiter' has in the books become the energizing power of the whole system" (1971, 598–9). Macfie says "there is no inconsistency" among the three invisible hands (596). In TMS and WN, the remarks speak tersely and obliquely to the momentous irregularity of existence, against the supreme regularity of nothingness.

On this way of seeing the remarks, Smith, then, is like the heathen savage—a likeness Smith was well aware of, I think. Both are invoking an invisible hand to explain the irregularity. Smith would not object. He expressed great admiration for "savage nations" (TMS 206.9). And at the outset of each of his two great works Smith makes self-deprecating remarks that should humble even the wisest of philosophers or scientists. Philosophy is an "antidote against fear and anxiety," as regards, perhaps, our future nonexistence, which might be what Smith means by "that awful futurity" that awaits us, but it is an antidote that is pursued "in vain" (TMS 12.11-12).

In the likeness between the heathen savage and Smith we may see an irony on Smith's part. But if so, it need not be a satirical sort of irony. We don't usually associate irony and sacredness, but maybe those two sentiments need not be strangers. Smith's love and admiration for God may have been like his love and admiration for science and philosophy, in regarding the highest articulated loop of the spiral with a sacredness but knowing full well that any such articulated loop emerges from things yet higher and deeper. In that way an irony may accompany that highest articulated loop. Knud Haakonssen (1981) says of the paragraph in TMS that immediately follows the invisible-hand paragraph: "In this passage, Smith strikes that perfect equipoise between irony and encomium which is so typical of him" (91). If Smith could strike a perfect equipoise between irony and encomium, perhaps he could do it also between irony and sacredness.

There is utility perhaps in enumerating the following points:

1. In TMS the invisible-hand paragraph is one of two sandwiched between the two longest paragraphs of the book (measured by word count), reflecting the intensity of that portion of the book.

2. That portion contains the parable of the poor man's son, the most dialectical segment of a highly dialectical work (Matson 2019).

3. There are remarkable textual connections between that portion and the most dramatic portion of Hume's *Treatise of Human Nature* (Matson and Doran 2017).

4. Indeed, in that part of TMS, there are a number of curious things about how Hume is represented (Matson, Doran, and Klein 2019).

5. The phrase "led by an invisible hand to" appears pretty exactly in the dead-center of the volumes containing the sixth edition of TMS and of the first edition of WN (Minowitz 2004, 404; Klein and Lucas 2011). In his rhetoric lectures, Smith noted that Thucydides "often expresses all that he labours so much in a word or two, sometimes placed in the middle of the narration" (LRBL 95).

6. In WN, the invisible-hand remark is practically the only one in the work that may be read as theistic

affirmation (Minowitz 2004, 408).

7.   An inclination toward irony is evidenced in Smith's first two publications, one on how "but by" consulting compiled passages in Samuel Johnson's *Dictionary* one may easily determine the way in which a word is used (see EPS 241), the other offering satirical praise for Rousseau's dedication to Geneva (see EPS 254).

8.   The *History of Astronomy*, where "the invisible hand of Jupiter" appears, arrives, in the final paragraph, at a surprise and irony about the interrelation between interpretation and factual belief (Matson 2018).

In TMS there are numerous exoteric affirmations of divine providence. One of the most wonderful mysteries surrounding Smith is the matter of his theism. I think a theism sustained by Smith would be one liberally tinged with irony (see TMS 167-70). To approach the irony in it all, allow me to relate material from Leo Rosten's *The Joys of Yiddish* (1968). Rosten's method is to introduce each Yiddish term, define it, and provide a story to illustrate it.

KALIKEH

Pronounced KOL-*li-keh* or KOLL-*yi-keh*, to rhyme with "doll yucca." Russian: "cripple."

1. Cripple

2. Someone who is sickly

3. A clumsy person

Mr. Katz fitted on the made-to-order suit and cried in dismay:

"Look at this sleeve! It's two inches too long!"

"So stick out your elbow," said the tailor, "which bends your arm—and the sleeve is just right!"

"The collar! It's half way up my head!"

"So raise your head up and back—and the collar goes down."

"But the left shoulder is two inches wider than the right!"

"So *bend*, this way, and it'll even out."

Mr. Katz left the tailor in this fantastic posture: right elbow stuck out wide, head far up and back, left shoulder tilted. A stranger accosted him.

"Excuse me, but would you mind giving me the name of your tailor?"

"*My* tailor?" Katz cried. "Are you mad? Why would anyone want my tailor?"

"Because any man who can fit a *kalikeh* like you is a genius!"

(Rosten 1968, 166-67)

Rosten's story may be used as an analogy about a period stretching from millions of years ago to today. Millions of years ago, "the tailor" presented a set of conditions. Over the eons our ancestors and their entire consciousness, "Mr. Katz," underwent innumerable adjustments in processes lost to time. The processes of adjustment, the starts and sallies of long evolution, are now, today, utterly unknown and little thought of by us today, the "stranger." And we may marvel at the genius of the Author of nature in fitting the world so suitably to universal benevolence.

Thus may the skeptic paint theism as evolved accretion. But the theist can embrace that evolutionary account, and marvel again at all that it presupposes, the great irregularity of existence. The skeptic can then incorporate his friend's marvel into his previous account, and so on without end.

CHAPTER 7

Adam Smith's Rebuke of the Slave Trade, 1759

Here and in the next chapter we consider two sentences in TMS, perhaps the most powerful passage in the work. In this chapter I consider the passage within the context of ideas that surround it. In the next chapter I contemplate the words of the passage itself.

The passage comes in Part V, titled: "Of the Influence of Custom and Fashion upon the Sentiments of Moral Approbation and Disapprobation." The Part is curiously meandering and enigmatic; the passage is the key to the whole Part. Once the passage is fully appreciated, the whole Part achieves cogency and power. It is quite clear that the two sentences, appearing in the original edition of 1759 and maintained thereafter, were an inspiration to the early antislavery movement.

Smith says that from the regularities of experience and practice "the imagination acquires a habit," and that such regularities—*custom* among the society in general, *fashion* among those "of a high rank, or character" (TMS 194.3)—may cause "many irregular and discordant opinions which prevail in different ages and nations concerning what is blamable or praise-worthy" (TMS 194.1). The Part consists of two chapters. The first considers clothing, furniture, architecture, and other such inanimate objects, and argues that, here, custom and fashion play a large role. Near the end of the chapter, he turns to fashions of the human form, and relates distant practices of foot-binding, ear elongation, and head-squaring of infants. He then writes:

> Europeans are astonished at the absurd barbarity of this practice, to which some missionaries have imputed the singular stupidity of those nations among whom it prevails. But when they condemn those savages, they do not reflect that the ladies in Europe had, till within these very few years, been endeavouring, for near a century past, to squeeze the beautiful roundness of their natural shape into a square form of the same kind. And that, notwithstanding the many distortions and diseases which this practice was known to occasion, **custom had rendered it agreeable among some of the most civilized nations which, perhaps, the world ever beheld.** (TMS 199.8, emphasis added)

The second chapter turns to the influence of custom and fashion "upon Moral Sentiments," that is, sentiments about the beauty or deformity of human conduct and character. Since the title of the entire Part speaks only of "Moral Approbation and Disapprobation," we may regard the first chapter, treating inanimate objects (or objects of non-moral sentiment) as warm-up.

Less malleable, these: The moral sentiments, "though they may be somewhat warpt, cannot be entirely perverted," for they "are founded on the strongest and most vigorous passions of human nature" (TMS 200.1). To the extent that moral standards do vary, they vary with circumstances. The variations follow different professions, different stages of life—young versus old—, and different stages of society—barbarism versus civilization and refinement.

Among "civilized nations," people cultivate especially the soft, amiable virtues, whereas in "rude and barbarous nations" people cultivate especially the respectable virtues of self-command. Smith employs the distinction between the amiable and the respectable virtues (TMS 23–26.1–10).

In a mammoth paragraph of 957 words,[1] Smith opens an extended, engrossing description of the "savages in North America," whose "magnanimity and self-command, in this respect, are almost beyond the conception of Europeans" (TMS 206.9). He embarks on a remarkable account of how they behave under great adversity and duress, including capture by their enemies, and protracted torture. The description is delivered calmly but it produces a bracing and sobering effect on the reader, inspiring a sense of awe. Smith continues the mammoth paragraph telling of their "song of death":

> Every savage is said to prepare himself, from his earliest youth, for this dreadful end: he composes for this purpose what they call the song of death, a song which he is to sing when he has fallen into the hands of his enemies, and is expiring under the tortures which they inflict upon him. It consists of insults upon his tormentors, and expresses the highest contempt of death and pain. He sings this song upon all extraordinary occasions; when he goes out to war, when he meets his enemies in the field, or whenever he has a mind to shew that he has familiarized his imagination to the most dreadful misfortunes, and that no human event can daunt his resolution or alter his purpose. (TMS 206.9)

At this point Smith turns the scene away from the native communities of North America: "The same contempt of death

---

1. The paragraph is the second longest when length is counted in terms of characters. When length is counted in terms of words, the paragraph is the third longest.

and torture prevails among all other savage nations"—

> There is not a negro from the coast of Africa who does
> not, in this respect, possess a degree of magnanimity
> which the soul of his sordid master is too often scarce
> capable of conceiving. Fortune never exerted more cru-
> elly her empire over mankind, than when she subject-
> ed those nations of heroes to the refuse of the jails of
> Europe, to wretches who possess the virtues neither of
> the countries which they come from, nor of those which
> they go to, and whose levity, brutality, and baseness, so
> justly expose them to the contempt of the vanquished.
> (TMS 206–7.9)

After these two sentences, appearing at the end of the mammoth
paragraph, Smith continues his original theme, as though nothing
has happened. But something has, and we must pause to reflect on
these two sentences.

The two sentences condemn slavery in general but aim especially at what was surely the most vicious "usage" that was being
practiced by some of the British readers' fellow Britons at the time
and voyaging from British ports: the slave trade. The first sentence
speaks of "the soul of his sordid master," but the signification is
vague, and it seems doubtful that Smith, sensitive to the compro-
mising positions that the status quo often places people in,[2] would
accuse every slaveholder of being sordid. The passage appears

2. "[T]here is often some unobserved circumstance which, if it was attended to, would
show us, that, independent of custom, there was a propriety in the character which custom had taught us to allot to each profession" (TMS 209.13). Smith's discussion of slavery
in *Lectures on Jurisprudence* shows that he saw dilemmas involved in undoing slavery: "a
generall insurrection would ensue," the slaves being "the naturall enemies of the governing
part" (LJ 187, 188).

as Smith writes of people of "rude and barbarous nations" (TMS 205.8). He speaks of "a negro from the coast of Africa." Most of the slaves in the American colonies in Smith's time were born and raised in the Americas.[3] To them, Smith's assumptions would not pertain. I regard the first sentence as an overture to the more definite condemnation of the second. What Smith means by "the refuse of the jails of Europe...wretches who possess the virtues neither of the countries which they come from, nor of those which they go to," are the slave traders, who show the virtues neither of England and other European countries which they come from (notably, the amiable virtues), nor of the African nations which they go to (notably, the respectable virtues of self-command); wretches whose actions "so justly expose them to the contempt of the vanquished."

Smith continues on with the theme into which the two sentences were inserted. He explains that "in civilized societies" people are more animated, expressive, amiable, as with "the French and the Italians": "An Italian, says the abbot Dû Bos, expresses more emotion on being condemned in a fine of twenty shillings, than an Englishman on receiving the sentence of death" (TMS 207.10). As for "animated eloquence," Smith says that it has been long practiced "both in France and Italy...but just beginning to be introduced into England. So wide is the difference between the degrees of self-command which are required in civilized and in barbarous nations...." (TMS 208.10).

Notice what Smith does: He exalts the self-command of the "savages" of North America and Africa. Next he draws a contrast

3. Between 1711 and 1760, the number of African slaves who survived the Middle Passage and disembarked on mainland North America was 175,789 (slavevoyages.org), and the number of slaves who ended up in North America after disembarking elsewhere would add perhaps a few tens of thousands of the slaves of 1760. Meanwhile, the US slave population in 1790 was 694,280 (1790 US Census). When Smith published his sentences in 1759, less than 35 percent had been born in Africa.

between the French/Italian and the English, with the English inferior in the amiable but superior in the respectable or "awful" virtues ("awful" meant *awesome* in Smith's day). The English retain a "rude" excellence in self-command. Smith arouses the Englishman's invidious pride against the French, enabling that contrast to extend itself backward to the engrossing mammoth paragraph that directly precedes the invidious European contrast. If the Englishman feels superior to the French, for superior English self-command, then, vastly superior yet are the vanquished Africans, "those nations of heroes." Smith uses English pride to arouse their sense of the sublime and to induce them to *look up to* the Africans, including those vanquished by European refuse. He paints for effect—in fact, the editors of TMS note that the abbot Jean-Baptiste Du Bos never said the specific thing Smith attributes to him (TMS 207.10 n2). Smith fabricated it, apparently, for effect.

And if the Englishman feels shame in his "rude" state of amiability, in that respect he may feel a sympathy with the deeper backwardness of those same vanquished souls. Smith induces all readers of the English-speaking world to identify with, to sympathize with, those over whom fortune never exerted her empire more cruelly.

After concluding his comparative discussion, Smith—87 percent of the way into Part V—comes, finally!, to a much more definite claim:

> All these effects of custom and fashion, however, upon the moral sentiments of mankind, are inconsiderable, in comparison of those which they give occasion to in some other cases; and it is not concerning the general style of character and behaviour, that those principles produce the greatest perversion of judgment, but concerning the propriety or impropriety of particular usages. (TMS 209.12)

Custom and fashion have less effect on conduct in general than on particular usages. "Usage" here means a particular practice, no matter how peculiar to outsiders, and stands in contrast to "the general style of character and behaviour" in the society. In the matter of society's general style of behavior, Smith goes on to say: "We expect truth and justice from an old man as well as from a young, from a clergyman as well as from an officer" (TMS 209.13). The rules of truth and justice are firm. Indeed, one of the major themes of TMS is "that remarkable distinction" (TMS 80.6) between commutative justice and all other virtues: Commutative justice—that is, "abstaining from what is another's" (TMS 269.10), or not messing with other people's stuff—is the only virtue whose rules are "precise and accurate," as opposed to "loose, vague, and indeterminate," thereby making the rules of commutative justice like those of grammar, whereas the rules of the other virtues are like the pointers and guidelines of aesthetic criticism (TMS 175.11; 327.1). Understand that in all this Smith is focusing on jural relationships "among equals" (TMS 80.7), and not on the governor-governed relationship.

However, Smith is saying that even such grammar-like rules can be grossly violated in "particular usages," or peculiar institutions. He now introduces an illustration from a much earlier era, discussed at length in another sizeable paragraph (528 words): infanticide in ancient Greece—"a practice allowed of in almost all the states of Greece, even among the polite and civilized Athenians." Indeed, Greece was viewed as the proud pinnacle of civilization. "This practice had, probably, begun in times of the most savage barbarity," but "[i]n the latter ages of Greece...the same thing was permitted from views of remote interest or conveniency, which could by no means excuse it" (TMS 210.15):

Uninterrupted custom had by this time so thoroughly
authorized the practice, that not only the loose max-
ims of the world tolerated this barbarous prerogative,
but even the doctrine of philosophers, which ought to
have been more just and accurate, was led away by the
established custom; and upon this, as upon many other occasions, instead of censuring, supported the horrible abuse by far-fetched considerations of public utility.
(TMS 210.15)

Smith here uses an intertemporal, as opposed to the previous
cross-sectional, comparison to play upon his reader's pride, who
may now be looking down on ancient Athens for its horrible practice. But how will future generations regard the horrible blots upon
our own current civilization? With what contempt will they regard
our "far-fetched considerations of public utility"?

Part V's next and final paragraph says that, although justice
might be trampled in particular usages, it cannot be trampled in
general by the citizens of a society (as opposed to by its governors),
and for "an obvious reason." The final paragraph is strikingly brief,
and, given the profound significance of the "obvious reason," ironic in its brevity:

There is an obvious reason why custom should never pervert our sentiments with regard to the general style and
character of conduct and behaviour, in the same degree
as with regard to the propriety or unlawfulness of particular usages. There never can be any such custom. No
society could subsist a moment, in which the usual strain
of men's conduct and behaviour was of a piece with the
horrible practice I have just now mentioned. (TMS 211.16)

The "obvious reason" is natural selection. A general respect among equals for commutative justice is "indispensable" (TMS, 175.11; see also 86.3–4), but when trampling is confined to particular usages, society can persist, as "with the horrible practice I have just now mentioned."

Well, the practice that Smith *just* now mentioned was infanticide in ancient Greece, a usage that, under certain ancient circumstances, Smith even seems willing to excuse (TMS 210.15; see also LJ 172–5, 449), and that, as David Hume had noted (1987, 399), was made legitimate by Solon, whom Smith takes as symbol of wise statesmanship (TMS 233.16; WN 543.53).

Indeed, the long paragraph on infanticide ends with the following words:

> When custom can give sanction to so dreadful a violation of humanity, we may well imagine that there is scarce any particular practice so gross which it cannot authorize. Such a thing, we hear men every day saying, is commonly done, and they seem to think this a sufficient apology for what, in itself, is the most unjust and unreasonable conduct. (TMS 210.15)

Just three pages prior, however, another horrible practice was mentioned, a "usage" that 365 days a year, day and night, visibly violated commutative justice and was for Smith's readers going on *right now*, voyaging from their own ports: the slave trade—a usage that "we hear men every day saying, is commonly done, and they seem to think this a sufficient apology." That was the horrible practice truly relevant—truly urgent.

Smith rebukes the slave trade not only when telling of slave traders being so justly exposed to the contempt of the vanquished but also when saying, in the Part's concluding words, that no society could "subsist a moment, in which the usual strain of men's conduct and behaviour was of a piece with the horrible practice I have just now mentioned." Indeed, Smith suggests that the perpetrators tend toward criminality, describing them as "the refuse of the jails of Europe." Heightening the intensity of the condemnation is the fact that it is the first time and nearly the only time in TMS that the reader finds Smith addressing a specific issue of current policy and declaiming upon it (Smith also rejects the illegality of suicide, TMS 287.34, and seems to endorse capital punishment, TMS 100.4).

An understanding of TMS should inform our reading of WN, and, specifically, Smith's rebuke in 1759 should inform our understanding of WN's discussion of slavery in 1776. There, Smith exposits slavery's economic inefficiency, but he never fulminates against its injustice.[4] But in 1759 Smith had announced (TMS 342.37) that he would augment his system with a work like WN; readers should understand that WN lives under the ethical umbrella of TMS. In TMS Smith introduces the illustration of infanticide as follows: "Can there be a greater barbarity, for example, than to hurt an infant?" (TMS 209.15). Perhaps there can—and Smith had spoken of it three pages earlier. Perhaps Smith felt that the sublimity of his rebuke in TMS would have been diminished by any new fulminations in WN about slavery being a great barbarity against natural liberty. In 1790, the year of Smith's death, in material added to the sixth and final edition of TMS, Smith speaks of domestic slavery as "the vilest of all states" and in the same paragraph speaks once again of how "an American savage prepares his death-song, and considers how he should act when he has fallen into the hands of his enemies, and is by them put to death in the most lingering

4. Smith discusses slavery in WN particularly at 98, 386–90, 587, 683–4, as well as extensively in *Lectures on Jurisprudence*, highlighting "the love of domination and tyrannizing" among slaveholders (p. 186); for analysis see Weingast (2020).

tortures, and midst the insults and derision of all the spectators" (TMS 282.28; see also 288.35).

Coming 28 years before the famed formation of the Society for Effecting the Abolition of the Slave Trade in 1787, Smith's 1759 rebuke was not lost on his contemporaries. In 1764, an anonymous antislavery pamphlet published in London quotes in full—and twice —Smith's two sentences.[5] That pamphlet is quoted by Thomas Clarkson in his classic two-volume account, *The History of the Rise, Progress, & Accomplishment of the Abolition of the African Slave-trade, by the British Parliament* (1808 I, 56-57)—the abolition act having been passed the previous year, in 1807. Clarkson writes that Adam Smith, one who "promoted the cause of the injured Africans...[,] had, so early as the year 1759, held them up in an honorable, and their tyrants in a degrading light," and then quotes in full the two sentences of Smith's rebuke (85–86). Clarkson then adds: "And... in 1776, in his Wealth of Nations, he showed in a forcible manner (for he appealed to the interest of those concerned) the dearness of African labor, or the impolicy of employing slaves" (86).

Also quoted in Clarkson's extensive honor roll are Francis Hutcheson (49) and John Millar (86–87). Millar (2006, 278–9) plainly echoes Smith: "Fortune perhaps never produced a situation more calculated to ridicule a liberal hypothesis." Clarkson writes: "It is a great honour to the university of Glasgow, that it should have produced, before any public agitation of this question, three professors, all of whom bore their public testimony against the continuance of the cruel trade" (87). In fact, the Glasgow line opposing slavery extends back also to Hutcheson's teacher, Gershom Carmi-

5. The pamphlet, *An Essay in Vindication of the Continental Colonies of America, from a Censure of Mr Adam Smith, in His "Theory of Moral Sentiments"* (1764) has been attributed to Arthur Lee. I have investigated the matter at considerable length, however, and have serious doubts about the attribution. The content of the pamphlet here is treated by Kendra Asher and me in chapter 9 in the present volume.

chael (2002, 140–145), making it four generations. Another Scottish professor honored and quoted by Clarkson is William Robertson of Edinburgh University (87–88). Also noticed by Clarkson (186) is Benjamin Rush, who in a pamphlet published in Philadelphia in 1773 also quotes in full Smith's two sentences (Rush 1773, 16–17, second pamphlet/pagination; see also 25). It is quite clear, then, that Smith's 1759 rebuke was an inspiration to the early movement against slavery and the slave trade. As for William Wilberforce, he admired Smith (though he disliked the Hume memorial; see Wilberforce 1797, 387), and quotes both of Smith's major works (1797, 105, 260, 262, 286; 1823, 2, 44, 48), though we find no reference to Smith's rebuke in particular.[6]

From moral theory and natural jurisprudence emerged liberal political economy. Its "liberal plan of equality, liberty, and justice" (WN 664.3) implied the emancipation of slaves and the undoing of privilege and caste generally, prompting Thomas Carlyle to dub it "the dismal science."

The anonymous pamphlet of 1764 concludes with the following words about Adam Smith: *"How had he bless'd mankind, and rescu'd me!"*

---

6. Also, Charles Sumner (1860, 2595) quotes Smith's two sentences in a speech in Congress (I thank Glory Liu for bringing this to my attention).

CHAPTER 8

The *Tao* Exposes Slavers to Contempt

T*he Theory of Moral Sentiments*, from the original of 1759, contains a passage condemning slavery. The second sentence zeros in on the slave-trade:

> There is not a negro from the coast of Africa who does not, in this respect, possess a degree of magnanimity which the soul of his sordid master is too often scarce capable of conceiving. Fortune never exerted more cruelly her empire over mankind, than when she subjected those nations of heroes to the refuse of the jails of Europe, to wretches who possess the virtues neither of the countries which they come from, nor of those which they go to, and whose levity, brutality, and baseness, so justly expose them to the contempt of the vanquished. (TMS 206–7)

The passage takes for granted self-ownership—the soul's ownership of its person—which, as Hume (2007, 488–490) indicated, constitutes the most native ownership and forms the template of the ownership principle. Smith, in his jurisprudence, spoke of how that principle gets "extended" to other objects (LJ 10, 16, 19-23, 27, 34, 38, 39, 207, 308, 309, 432. 434, 460, 466, 467, 468).

In the preceding chapter, I write about the slave-trade passage in relation to the surrounding text. Smith leads British readers into identifying with the respectable persons shackled by slavers from Britain and elsewhere in Europe. Smith indicates that "No society could subsist a moment, in which the usual strain of men's conduct and behaviour was of a piece with the horrible practice" of slavery (TMS 211).

Here I remark on the wording within the passage.

The first sentence moves the scene from the Americas to Africa, to illustrate anew the contrast between polished and "savage" cultures. The interaction taken up is a practice, Hume noted in 1752, "which has been abolished for some centuries throughout the greater part of Europe" (1985, 383). Slavery had been largely abolished in western Christendom, only to be reintroduced in the colonies in the Americas.

The first sentence sets up the second sentence. But there is a word in the first sentence that quietly moves toward the sublime, and that word is *soul.* Smith speaks of "the soul of his sordid master."

In the first chapter of TMS, Smith uses "soul." When we look upon the dead we lodge "our own living souls in their inanimated bodies" (TMS 13.13). But Smith uses "soul" only in a handful of other instances throughout the remainder of the book, and several of those come in his presentation of ancient thought. Yet Smith's affirmation of the soul should not be in doubt.

By lodging our soul in the inanimate we may discover the sublime. Hear again the second sentence:

> Fortune never exerted more cruelly her empire over mankind, than when she subjected those nations of heroes to the refuse of the jails of Europe, to wretches who possess the virtues neither of the countries which they come from, nor of those which they go to, and

whose levity, brutality, and baseness, so justly expose them to the contempt of the vanquished.

The sentence stands out for its animisms. First, there is Fortune —*Fortuna*—which exerts her empire. She subjects heroes to being vanquished. Moreover, she does so "cruelly." In TMS, Smith is not shy to animate the inanimate, but imbuing the animistic spirit with a mien such as cruelty is striking. It makes one think of the start of Smith's famous parable of the poor man's son, "whom heaven in its anger has visited with ambition" (TMS 181.8). Heaven is angry, and *Fortuna* is cruel.

The end of the sentence takes animism yet higher. The slavers' levity, brutality, and baseness expose them to the contempt of the vanquished, and "so justly."

In pondering "justly," I had once thought in terms of the vanquished individuals' estimating of the slavers: Their contempt was estimatively just.

But rather than it being the vanquished who act justly, perhaps it is another animistic spirit. Levity, brutality, and baseness expose the slavers to contempt: Such moral operations are actively sustained by the moral order. In *The Abolition of Man*, originally published in 1944, C.S. Lewis called it the *Tao*. And in sustaining such operations the *Tao* acts justly. The sort of justice here is distributive: The *Tao* makes a becoming use of what is its own. The *Tao* exposes justly. C.S. Lewis wrote another book, *Miracles*; the twelfth chapter is "The Propriety of Miracles." The *Tao* is proprietous.

And notice a difference in verb tense. Fortune "exerted," it "subjected"—past tense—whereas the elements of the *Tao* "expose" — present tense. The slavers continue to be exposed to the contempt of the vanquished. Those trepanned and shackled are vanquished in their bodies—but not in their souls.

The contempt rings in eternity, but also it is rung anew again and again, perennially, today and in all future days. A new ally of the vanquished is born each day.

The *Tao* will continue to expose its enemies to contempt. Smith told tyrants: Your levity, brutality, and baseness justly expose you to contempt. You, beyond reasonable call, control people, take their stuff, restrict their liberty, rather than leaving them to act peaceably of their own accord, to pursue their own interests their own way. But you shall not escape the contempt that your levity, brutality, and baseness so richly earn you.

CHAPTER 9

Raillery of Adam Smith: Praise-by-Blame by a 1764 Pamphlet on Slavery

by Daniel Klein and Kendra Asher

In 1764 there appeared in London an anonymous pamphlet, *An Essay in Vindication of the Continental Colonies of America, from A Censure of Mr Adam Smith, in his Theory of Moral Sentiments. With some Reflections on Slavery in General.* The title page says "By an AMERICAN." The pamphlet has often been misunderstood by modern scholars. On the surface the pamphlet rebuts Adam Smith for a passage in TMS—the famous passage condemning the slave trade. But the pamphlet misconstrues the passage as Smith censuring American colonists as base "wretches" and the "refuse of the jails of Europe."

It is clear that Smith was referring principally to slave ship crews, who often had spent time in jails or faced imprisonment. The pamphlet's true intent was to honor Smith and to promote his rebuke of the slave-trade and slavery in general. Also, the misconstrual of Smith satirizes the miscommunication and misunderstanding between the American colonies and Britain, a problem made inevitable by the ocean between them.

The feigned misconstrual leads the reader into the final 40 percent of the pamphlet, where the text suddenly launches into an all-out condemnation of slavery. Indeed, the pamphlet was recognized as such by the American abolitionist Anthony Benezet and the chronicler of the anti-slave-trade movement Thomas Clarkson.

Authorship of the pamphlet has been attributed to Arthur Lee. We doubt that attribution and suppose that the invisible hands behind the pamphlet were British satirists of the day. In future work we will explain why we are convinced that the author of *Essay in Vindication* was not Arthur Lee and speculate about the identity of the true authors. We discuss the pamphlet in greater detail in a scholarly article at *American Political Thought* (Klein and Asher 2022).

In the TMS passage, original to the 1759 first edition, the first sentence sneakily leads the reader into the subject of slavery; it sets up the second sentence:

> There is not a negro from the coast of Africa who does not, in this respect, possess a degree of magnanimity which the soul of his sordid master is scarce capable of conceiving. Fortune never exerted more cruelly her empire over mankind, than when she subjected those nations of heroes to the refuse of the jails of Europe, to wretches who possess the virtues neither of the countries which they come from, nor of those which they go to, and whose levity, brutality and baseness, so justly expose them to the contempt of the vanquished. (TMS 206-207)

The sublime passage is reproduced in full not once but twice in the 1764 pamphlet supposedly written by "an AMERICAN." Smith's passage was significant in advancing the movement against slavery and the slave-trade.

At that time, anonymous satirical writing was common.

Edmund Burke's first major publication, *A Vindication of Natural Society* (1756), was anonymous and satirical. He wrote to Elizabeth Montagu in 1763, six months prior to the publication of *Essay in Vindication*:

> Madam I observe that Panegyric, even when applied to those who deserve it most or like it best is sure never to please above one, and will certainly offend fifty. To say the truth Satyr is now so much the safer and (what is now the only rule of right) the more popular way, that I am resolved to stick to that…. (29 July 1763, in Burke 1958, 171)

The pamphlet was produced in that same spirit. The satire was directed at the type of person who could possibly misconstrue Smith's words.

But the pamphlet is also a raillery of Adam Smith. In his book on the use of irony from 1500 to 1755, Norman Knox (1961) explains that one type of raillery "was praise-by-blame irony; under the clever hand of the rallier mock faults turned into real virtues and mock ridicule turned into real praise" (196). Jonathan Swift explained, "Raillery was to say something that at first appeared a reproach or reflection; but, by some turn of wit unexpected and surprising, ended always in a compliment, and to the advantage of the person it was addressed to" (Swift as quoted in Knox 1961, 198, 203).

The pamphlet pretends to defend American colonists from unjust censure by Smith. The first 60 percent takes for granted that Smith censured American colonists as "refuse of the jails of Europe." The final 40 percent of the Essay, however, is a full-scale assault on slavery. The end of the *Essay* returns to the ruse with which the pamphlet began, and with an irony that is quite evident once one

FIG. 9.1: *IN VINDICATION* **TITLE PAGE WITH INSCRIPTION**

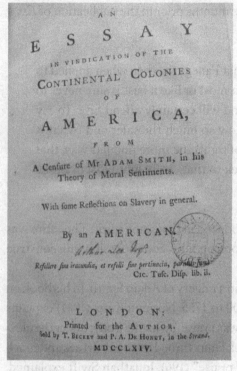

AN

ESSAY

IN VINDICATION OF THE

CONTINENTAL COLONIES

OF

AMERICA,

FROM

A Censure of Mr ADAM SMITH, in his
Theory of Moral Sentiments.

With some Reflections on Slavery in general.

By an AMERICAN.

Arthur Lee Esq?

Refellere sine iracundia, et refelli sine pertinacia, parati sumus.
Cic. Tusc. Disp. lib. ii.

LONDON:

Printed for the AUTHOR,
Sold by T. BECKET and P. A. DE HONDT, in the *Strand*.
MDCCLXIV.

Source: Bodleian Libraries, University of Oxford, G.Pamph. 296.

has traced the satirical thread.

The second sentence of Smith's passage is clearly aimed at the slave-trade: "Fortune never exerted more cruelly her empire over mankind, than when she subjected those nations of heroes to **the refuse of the jails of Europe, to wretches who possess the virtues neither of the countries which they come from, nor of those which they go to,** and whose levity, brutality and baseness, so justly expose them to the contempt of the vanquished" (emphasis added).

John Newton was the slave ship master who later in life turned abolitionist and wrote the song "Amazing Grace"; he was portrayed in the 2006 film *Amazing Grace*. In an unpublished letter of 1752 about mastering slave ships Newton wrote: "We are for the most part supplied with the refuse and dregs of the nation. The prisons and glass houses furnish us with large quotas and boys impatient of their parents and masters, or already ruined by some untimely vice and for the most part devoid of all good principles" (Newton 1962, xiv). It is striking that Newton in 1752 speaks of the "refuse" from "prisons" while in 1759 Smith writes of "the refuse of the jails of Europe." Scholarship on the slave ship crews makes clear that many of the crewmen had come from jails or faced imprisonment, often because scheming "crimpers," working with the slavers, ensnared wayward young men into a situation of having to choose between imprisonment and signing away their debt by signing on to a slave ship voyage (Christopher 2006, 31–32; Rediker 2007, 225–228).

Smith's description clearly would *not* fit an American slaveholder, for the colonists were, with few exceptions, not from the jails of Europe and did not come from one country *and go to another*—and, especially, not to another that differs sharply in social morals. Plainly, it is the slave traders who were the "wretches," lacking the virtues of the lands traversed.

The pamphlet's ruse may have served another purpose: To highlight misunderstandings between the American colonists and the political class in London. The pamphlet appeared about two months before the Sugar Act was passed on 5 April, 1764. The next year saw the Stamp Act. In 1775 Burke explained in his Speech on Conciliation with the Colonies: "[I]t is not merely moral, but laid deep in the natural constitution of things. Three thousand miles of ocean lie between you and them. No contrivance can prevent the effect of this distance in weakening government. Seas roll, and months pass, between the order and the execution; and the want of a speedy explanation of a single point is enough to defeat a whole system" (Edmund Burke 1999, 242). He reminds British Parliamentarians: "Your children do not grow faster from infancy to manhood, than [the Americans] spread from families to communities, and from villages to nations" (228). Miscommunications and animosities are quite inevitable: "[C]onsider, I implore you, that the communication by special messages, and orders between these agents and their constituents on each variation of the case, when the parties come to contend together, and to dispute on their relative proportions, will be a matter of delay, perplexity, and confusion that never can have an end" (282).

The remoteness of North America made it impossible for the British to do much more than practice benign neglect and enjoy free trade with the colonies. To attempt to extract much in taxation would generate misunderstandings, suspicion, and hostility. The pamphlet's satirical misconstrual of the North Briton's words by "an AMERICAN" may have played upon troubles in understanding between Britain and the colonies, stemming from "the natural constitution of things." If so, the satire could be said to have had the compounded purposes of ending the slave-trade, abolishing slavery, avoiding war, and pushing a speedier independence for the American colonies.

CHAPTER 10

Classical Liberalism: A Short Introduction

L iberty is central to classical liberals. It may be summarized
as person, property, and consent, the individual's dominion
that others are presumptively not to mess with. Here is a
short introduction to classical liberalism, with the United States
in mind.

Suppose your neighbor asserts that he is to get 25 percent of your
income and brandishes a gun to show that he means business. Or,
suppose he says you are not to employ people for less than a certain
wage, or that you can hire only plumbers on his own special list of
plumbers. We'd consider such a neighbor to be criminal in initiating such coercions. Classical liberals say it's coercion when done
by government, too. Yes, government is a special sort of player in
society; its coercions differ from those of criminals. Its coercions
are overt, institutionalized, openly rationalized, even supported
by a large portion of the public. They are called intervention or
restriction or regulation or taxation, rather than extortion, assault,
theft, or trespass. But they are still initiations of coercion. That
is important, because recognizing it helps sustain a presumption
against government coercions, a presumption of liberty. Classical
liberals think that many extant interventions do not, in fact, meet
the burden of proof for overcoming the presumption. Many interventions should be rolled back, repealed, abolished.

Liberalization

Thus, classical liberals favor liberalizing social affairs. That goes as a general presumption: For business, work, and trade, but also for guns and for "social" issues, such as drugs, sex, speech, and voluntary association. That presumption differentiates the classical liberals from both those who readily favor "economic" restrictions and those who readily favor "moral" restrictions.

Classical liberals favor smaller government. Government operations, such as schools, rely on taxes or privileges (and sometimes user fees). Even apart from the coercive nature of taxation, classical liberals don't like the governmentalization of social affairs, for its unhealthy moral and cultural effects. They favor school-choice reforms and lean against redistribution and the welfare state.

Classical liberals can be radicals, believing in liberty as a sort of logos and axiom. Some ponder a pure-liberty destination. But *classical liberal* is suitable to describe an attitude that respects the status quo and yet looks to liberalize, that has a directional tendency to augment liberty, even if reforms are small or moderate. So classical liberals can be moderate or radical, directional or destinational. They can bargain, or they can challenge.

Overall liberty

Most classical liberals recognize that sometimes liberty must be sacrificed for the sake of liberty. A policy that reduces liberty directly might augment liberty overall. Areas of contention among classical liberals include immigration, foreign policy, weapons policy, pollution, and financial doings for which the taxpayer is on the hook.

Here, we might have a way to interpret some of the differences between classical liberals and conservatives who also cherish liberty: Classical liberals sometimes think that conservatives overstate disagreement between direct and overall liberty, and conservatives sometimes think classical liberals overstate agreement. Conservatives are often more favorable than classical liberals to, say, restricting immigration or enhancing military spending.

In the United States, the word *conservative* functions widely as code for Republican. Conservatives feel more involved in the contest for power. Classical liberals sometimes come across as theoreticians who don't concern themselves with the struggle for power and the process of actually making reforms. They are accused of being content to espouse liberalization yet failing to help bring it about. Classical liberals might respond by saying that insight and understanding are a precondition to reform, and that research and learning are crucial to wise leadership.

The principle of liberty has its holes, gray areas, and exceptions; it does not speak to all important issues of government; and it is not self-justifying. Despite the limitations, however, it remains cogent and gives backbone to classical liberal thought.

Liberalism unrelinquished

The first political meaning of the word *liberal* was launched in the 1770s, most notably by Adam Smith. But in the period 1880 to 1940, many English words lost or changed meanings, including the political term *liberal*. In the postwar period, classical liberal ideas enjoyed some reinvigoration, led by such figures as Friedrich Hayek and Milton Friedman, now sometimes fashioned as *libertarian*, notably by Murray Rothbard, who offered up a sort of paradigm of libertarianism. The term *libertarian* can function as signification both for the more formulaic thinking of Rothbard and for the less formulaic thinking.

America has an election system in which third parties damage their own cause—because it is predominantly a two-party system. For this reason, many libertarians and classical liberals do not support the Libertarian Party. The small size of the Libertarian Party should not be taken to mark the extent of classical liberal sentiment. Many classical liberal sympathizers do not vote at all, vote Republican, or vote Democratic. Outside the Washington-DC Beltway, most self-described classical liberals think, as I do, that Republicans are the lesser evil.

CHAPTER 11

Oren Cass Balderdash on Adam Smith

O ren Cass leads American Compass, a website that seeks to influence the Republican Party, and has there published a long article that recounts the development of his thought (2022a). Once Cass was a "convert to a fundamentalist sect," namely "market fundamentalism." Now he has matured and opposes something called "globalization," which is the "antithesis" of "capitalism." Capitalism, we learn, "locks everyone in a room together and encourages them to find a way out."

Throughout the maturation process, however, he has felt that he had Adam Smith by his side. He still invokes Smith. Unfortunately for Cass, the invocation is ungrounded. As we shall see, Cass particularly misrepresents Smith on matters of foreign investment.

Cass's views revolve around an idea of a "bounded market," where "economic analysis and legal treatment of activity depends on whether it occurs within the boundary, across it, or beyond it." He says of a "bounded market": "Through restrictions on trade or capital flows, public policy can force imports and exports into balance, so that goods and services are exchanged for each other rather than for financial instruments" (2022a).

But a bounded market already exists, as Dominic Pino (2022) points out. Pino explains that Cass's sloganeering simply spells yet more governmentalization of social affairs. In doing so, Cass is at odds with Adam Smith. Yet Cass insists otherwise. He concedes that Smith and David Ricardo taught that free enterprise generally advances the good of the whole. But Cass has made a discovery: "Their theories applied, they both insisted, only so long as a nation's capitalists invested within its own borders." Donald Boudreaux (2022) has treated Cass's invocation of Ricardo. Here I focus on his invocation of Smith.

The first chapter of Smith's *Wealth of Nations* (23.11) culminates in marvel and wonder: "How much commerce and navigation in particular, how many ship-builders, sailors, sail-makers, rope-makers, must have been employed in order to bring together the different drugs made use of by the dyer, which often come from the remotest corners of the world!"

That exclamation point is one of three at the end of three consecutive sentences. Here, Smith imagines the worldwide activities flowing into the woolen coat enjoyed by "the most common artificer or day-labourer" (WN 22.11). Beyond that chapter, there are only three exclamation points in *Wealth of Nations*. Smith, then, begins his work with a unique sense of marvel at how his theories *do* apply across national boundaries.

Smith wrote: "[E]ach nation ought, not only to endeavour itself to excel, but from the love of mankind, to promote, instead of obstructing the excellence of its neighbours" (TMS 229.3). Smith's ethics are patterned after benevolent monotheism and a universalistic Imago Dei: "The all-wise Author of Nature," he says in *The Theory of Moral Sentiments*, "has made man, if I may say so, the immediate judge of mankind; and has in this respect, as in many others, created him after his own image" (TMS 128–130.31). He calls the Chinese the "brethren" of Europeans.

Whereas Cass wants to see public policy "force imports and exports into balance," Smith wrote: "Nothing, however, can be more absurd than this whole doctrine of the balance of trade" (WN 488.2). Boudreaux and I (2017) have explained a rival semantic wherein what is normally expressed as a "trade deficit" is a "current-stuff surplus." Smith's free-trade teaching rings out in *Wealth of Nations* (notable spots include 448, 538–539, 629, 637).

In economic affairs that cross national boundaries, people benefit one another not only by navigation and trade. They do so also by investment, as when an Englishman invests in enterprises in France, or a Frenchman invests in enterprises in England. In Cass's mind, foreign investment is something baneful. His "bounded market" seems to say that the government should further restrict, if not prohibit, foreign investment.

On the matter of foreign investment, Cass misrepresents Smith in two ways. First, he seems to suggest that Smith's theorizing assumes that there is little to no foreign investment. Cass writes, "Smith and Ricardo…assumed that capital would remain in the domestic market. And as a corollary, both conceived of trade as occurring only on the basis of goods for goods." In a reply to Pino, Cass (2022b) writes: "Smith and Ricardo wrote about one very specific kind of trade—the direct exchange of goods for goods— and assumed this would occur in a world where capital remained within national boundaries."

Second, Cass suggests that Smith's favor for liberal policy depended on such an assumption of little to no foreign investment. Cass writes: "Smith and Ricardo never suggest that this pursuit of profit abroad will align with the public interest at home, no other theory gives a reason that it should, and empirically it has not" (2022a).

On both points, Cass is wrong about Smith. I do not mean to imply that under no circumstances would Smith favor a restriction on foreign trade or investment. Smith considered arguments for making an exception to the principle of free trade, but, as Boudreaux (2020) explains, Smith himself tended to diminish those arguments. We cannot rule out that Smith might favor certain restrictions under certain circumstances, for polity reasons, perhaps because they would support political stability or national security, or simply because they would play a part in the crafty art of liberal politics. Smith strove to make governments less dishonest and illiberal, but knew that foreign countries had governments, too. Smith's friend Edmund Burke exemplified the virtuous pursuit of circumstantial liberal politics.

Smith said that foreign investment tended not to be extensive because, when an Englishman is deciding where to invest, a domestic enterprise holds natural advantages over a foreign enterprise. But the outcome is something that occurs naturally under liberal policy:

> [E]very individual endeavours to employ his capital as near home as he can, and consequently as much as he can in the support of domestic industry; **provided always that he can thereby obtain the ordinary, or not a great deal less than the ordinary profits of stock.**
>
> Thus, **upon equal or nearly equal profits**, every wholesale merchant naturally prefers the home-trade to the foreign trade of consumption, and the foreign trade of consumption to the carrying trade. In the home-trade his capital is never so long out of his sight as it frequently is in the foreign trade of consumption. He can know better the character and situation of the persons whom he trusts, and if he should happen to be deceived, he knows better the laws of the country from which he must seek redress. (WN 454.6; emphasis added)

Smith is saying that the natural advantages of staying close to home make up for a little less in expected "profits." But that is not to say that those natural advantages will necessarily compensate for a *lot* less in expected profits. If the opportunity in France promises substantially more, maybe our Englishman invests there. It is unusual for an Englishman to know and seize such a French opportunity, rather than a Frenchman. But Smith does not rule out the possibility. Maybe our Englishman has family or friends in France, or business associates that he has come to trust.

Smith reckoned investment in "the carrying trade"—that is, shipping between countries other than the investor's own country—as something other than domestic investment, saying: "In the carrying trade, the capital of the merchant is, as it were, divided between two foreign countries, and no part of it is ever necessarily brought home, or placed under his own immediate view and command." Wealthy men in a rich country often invest in the carrying trade:

> When the capital stock of any country is increased to such a degree, that it cannot be all employed in supplying the consumption, and supporting the productive labour of that particular country, the surplus part of it naturally disgorges itself into the carrying trade, and is employed in performing the same offices to other countries. The carrying trade is the natural effect and symptom of great national wealth; but it does not seem to be the natural cause of it…. Holland, in proportion to the extent of the land and the number of its inhabitants, by far the richest country in Europe, has, accordingly, the greatest share of the carrying trade of Europe. (WN 373.35)

Smith also recognizes foreign investment by the British in "the stores and warehouses from which goods are retailed in some provinces, particularly in Virginia and Maryland" (WN 367.21). Smith regrets how British policy has blocked investment into the colonies from countries other than Britain: "[B]y the expulsion of all foreign capitals [the monopoly on colonial trade] necessarily reduced the whole quantity of capital employed in that trade below what it naturally would have been in the case of free trade" (WN 598.25).

And Smith discussed the East India Company extensively. He thought it dependent on bailouts from the British state and abusive of Indians. Its exclusive monopoly should lapse. It was the Company's exclusive privilege and abuse that Smith opposed, not trade and investment. Smith called for "the trade to be laid open to all the subjects of the state [Britain]" (WN 598.25).

Does Smith ever frown on foreign investment? Smith does say that British capital invested in Britain more surely augments employment in Britain than British capital invested abroad. But universal benevolence does not stop at the border: "The capitals of the British manufacturers who work up the flax and hemp annually imported from the coasts of the Baltic, are surely very useful to the countries which produce them" (WN 365.17). Smith hardly seems opposed to British investment in the Baltic countries. Elsewhere Smith writes: "Though the same capital never will maintain the same quantity of productive labour in a distant as in a near employment, yet a distant employment may be as necessary for the welfare of the society as a near one; the goods which the distant employment deals in being necessary, perhaps, for carrying on many of the nearer employments" (WN 629.87).

Smith's point about the advantages of investing close to home leads into the invisible-hand passage in *Wealth of Nations*:

By preferring the support of domestic to that of foreign industry, he intends only his own security; and by directing that industry in such a manner as its produce may be of the greatest value, he intends only his own gain, and he is in this, **as in many other cases, led by an invisible hand to** promote an end which was no part of his intention. (WN 456.9; emphasis added)

Quoting the passage, Cass suggests that Smith wishes to confine the invisible-hand point to when the individual invests domestically, writing: "If a capitalist wishes to deploy his capital domestically, and if the domestic investment that will generate the most profit for him is also the one that will create the most value and employ the most people in his country, *then* we will have a well-functioning capitalist system" (2022a). I take it that Cass means *only then*.

But to think that Smith confines the invisible-hand idea thusly is daft. As Peter Minowitz (2004, 384–385) has shown when criticizing a similar misreading, the invisible-hand idea is all over *Wealth of Nations*. Minowitz's textual analysis refutes Cass's attempt to confine the point.

It makes more sense to think that Smith, in propounding a presumption of liberty, assured readers and lawmakers that liberalizations will not lead to an exodus of capital and widespread disruptions of economic life. Smith is saying: Don't worry, the investor who is free to choose will usually choose domestic anyway.

Cass motivates his slogans in part as protecting American jobs and securing livelihoods. Smith addressed the issue of how freeing up international trade might put people in outcompeted businesses out of work. What did Smith propose?

Soldiers and seamen, indeed, when discharged from the king's service, are at liberty to exercise any trade, within any town or place of Great Britain or Ireland. Let the same natural liberty of exercising what species of industry they please, be restored to all his majesty's subjects, in the same manner as to soldiers and seamen; that is, break down the exclusive privileges of corporations, and repeal the statute of apprenticeship, both which are real encroachments upon natural liberty, and add to these the repeal of the law of settlements, so that a poor workman, when thrown out of employment either in one trade or in one place, may seek for it in another trade or in another place, without the fear either of a prosecution or of a removal, and neither the public nor the individuals will suffer much more from the occasional disbanding some particular classes of manufacturers, than from that of soldiers. (WN 470.42)

Of Cass's slogans, Smith would say: "Every such regulation introduces some degree of real disorder into the constitution of the state, which it will be difficult afterwards to cure without occasioning another disorder" (WN 472.44).

As Pino (2022) writes: "If Cass is unhappy with the results of the bounded market we have, perhaps he'd be open to making the government a little less powerful instead." Cass might help liberalize any of the 10,000 commandments now obstructing gainful employment and honest living. Then Cass could justly invoke Adam Smith.

CHAPTER 12

What's Natural about Adam Smith's Natural Liberty?

By Daniel Klein and Erik Matson

A bundantly does Adam Smith use "liberty" in *The Wealth of Nations.* "Liberty" usually means "allowing every man to pursue his own interest his own way" (WN 664.3). Smith sometimes adds an adjective, as in "perfect liberty" or "general liberty."

And then there is "natural liberty," which appears ten times. Ten is not a huge number. In fact, there are more occurrences of "perfect liberty"—sixteen. But the occurrences of "natural liberty" are significant. Most famous are those in the penultimate paragraph of Book IV:

> All systems either of preference or of restraint, therefore, being thus completely taken away, the obvious and simple system of **natural liberty** establishes itself of its own accord. Every man, as long as he does not violate the laws of justice, is left perfectly free to pursue his own interest his own way, and to bring both his industry and capital into competition with those of any other man, or order of men. The sovereign is completely discharged from a duty, in the attempting to perform which he must always be exposed to innumerable delusions, and for

the proper performance of which no human wisdom or
knowledge could ever be sufficient; the duty of superin-
tending the industry of private people, and of directing
it towards the employments most suitable to the interest
of the society. According to the system of **natural liberty**,
the sovereign has only three duties to attend to.... (WN
687.51, emphasis added)

Four occurrences of "natural liberty" come when Smith points
out that in endorsing a restriction on banks against issuing small-de-
nomination notes he is making an exception to the principle of natural liberty: "But those exertions of the natural liberty of a few individuals, which might endanger the security of the whole society,
are, and ought to be, restrained by the laws of all governments; of
the most free, as well as of the most despotical" (WN 324.94).

Another comes in his outburst against the Settlement Act: "To
remove a man who has committed no misdemeanour from the
parish where he chuses to reside, is an evident violation of natural liberty and justice" (WN 157.59). Another comes in a remark:
"Both laws were evident violations of natural liberty, and therefore
unjust" (WN 530.16). And two come when he says that repealing
"encroachments upon natural liberty" would ease the readjustment
of those put out of work by free trade (WN 470.42).

In all ten cases, "natural liberty" means the flipside of commutative justice. Commutative justice is not messing with others' person, property, and promises-due, and the flipside is others—including the government—not messing with one's own such stuff. Smith
pegs natural liberty as the flipside of commutative justice when he
says "[b]oth laws were violations of natural liberty and **therefore**
unjust" (WN 530.16, emphasis added). Smith often said simply "liberty" but sometimes "natural liberty."

WHAT'S NATURAL ABOUT ADAM SMITH'S NATURAL LIBERTY? 93

Why did Smith sometimes say "natural liberty"? Maybe he wanted to highlight its "naturalness." That prompts the question: What is "natural" about Smith's "natural liberty"?

"Nature" and "natural" loom large in Smith. The words feature in the full titles of his two published works: *An Inquiry into the Nature and Causes of the Wealth of Nations* and *The Theory of Moral Sentiments, or An Essay towards an Analysis of the Principles by which Men naturally judge concerning the Conduct and Character, first of their Neighbours, and afterwards of themselves.*[1] But the meaning of "nature" eludes simple definition. According to A.L. Macfie (1967), "Smith's 'Nature' is like Heinz's tins—there are fifty-seven varieties" (7).

The polysemy of "nature" and its cognates was well known. David Hume claimed there is no word "more ambiguous and unequivocal" than "nature" and offered three (among many) possible definitions: that which is opposed to miracles, that which is opposed to the rare and unusual, and that which is opposed to artifice (Hume 2007, 304–5). Samuel Johnson, in his *Dictionary of the English Language*, lists thirteen definitions of "nature," along with eight of "natural."

In TMS Smith sometimes plays different ideas of nature off one another, telling how "man is by Nature directed to correct, in some measure, that distribution of things which she herself would otherwise have made" (TMS 168.9). Our natural moral sentiments often lead us to strive against aspects of "nature," or the way things usually are in the world. Tyranny, domination, monopoly, and coercion are natural, and, naturally, we rail against them (cf. Brubaker 2006; Pack 1995).

Let's focus on "natural." Here are four definitions that advance a Smithian understanding:

1. The full title of TMS has become obscured, in large part because the editors of the Glasgow variorum edition chose to use the abbreviated title, against Smith's own designation from the fourth edition onwards.

1. Existing in the primeval human state, with only primitive language, the most basic forms of property, and no subordination to a political body. Making a contrast with "artificial," which itself has multiple senses, Hume said: "Sucking is an action natural to Man, and Speech is artificial" (published in back matter of Hume 2007, 430).

2. Usual or expected as in "the natural and ordinary state of mankind" (TMS 45.7).

3. Necessary for the state of human affairs that the speaker presupposes or posits.

4. Worth naturalizing, which is to say, worth actualizing such that we get to a state of affairs in which the thing we say is natural would then be expected (sense 2) or necessary (sense 3). Beneficial.

There are yet other meanings of "natural" in Smith,[2] among which we could include:

- essential or definitionally necessary;
- resultant from human action but not human design, as in natural versus artificial (here we have a second sense of "artificial");
- not resultant from actions of superior beings, as in natural versus supernatural.

Also, in WN we have "natural" price/wage/rent/rate/proportion/balance and so on. These sometimes relate to expected or necessary; also, sometimes, they might be thought of as outcomes obtaining under a certain set of hypothetical assumptions,

2. Charles Griswold (1999, 311–17) lists seven.

as in an equilibrium model.

But put these other meanings aside, and let us continue with the enumerated four senses.

These four senses launch a dynamic. Evolution generated "man," in his primeval state, which might be associated with the end of the environment of evolutionary adaptedness, namely small bands at the end of the Paleolithic Age (10,000 BC). The primeval state is, in Smith, the hunter stage of social development.

Once man—and hence man-in-society—has been posited, whether primeval or beyond, there operates a recursive dynamic of senses 2, 3, and 4. In the Neolithic Age, with agriculture and settlement, new practices and structures develop; new regularities in social life develop and become expected and therefore natural (sense 2). People also become aware of different societies with different regularities, or of changes in their own society over time, and see that preconditions are necessary to arrive at and sustain certain social arrangements (sense 3).

Finally, a sense of the common good—in us since the primeval and natural in all four senses—looks to improvement; certain practices thought to advance the good are endorsed. They are thought to be potentialities that *ought to be actualized* (sense 4). Should they be actualized, they become natural in senses 2 and 3. Sense 4 is "natural" in its *becoming* sense.

With the four definitions in mind, we again ask: What's natural about Smith's natural liberty?

Even in the primeval state, we have ownership of our person and immediate possessions. David Friedman (1994) affirms that we have "natural property" in our own person, by virtue of a special knowledge and control of it, and our mutual recognition of one another's spheres of knowledge and control. Bart Wilson argues similarly in *The Property Species: Mine, Yours, and the Human Mind*

(2020), saying that "no human parents in any community have to teach their child to resist attempts to take things securely within their grasp. Children are natural-born possessors" (9). Wilson propounds the idea that we naturally "emphysicalize the concept of mine" (15), a concept that starts with the most personal of objects, our own mind and our own body. Hume affirmed the special relationship we have in the "fix'd and constant advantages of the mind and body" (Hume 2007, 314).

Thus, there is self-ownership in the primeval state. Indeed, hunter-gatherer bands did not have the hierarchy and technology to enslave. A band that did not accord its members self-ownership simply would not survive. A band is best thought of as an association of jural equals. The vision is also true to Smith on the hunter stage.

When Smith then moves to the more advanced stages, of shepherds, of agriculture, and of commerce, he says that property is *extended* (LJ 10, 16, 19–23, 27, 34, 38, 39, 207, 308, 309, 432, 434, 460, 466, 467, 468). Property in one's own person is primevally natural, and the principle is subsequently extended to objects that in the primeval state had not yet been propertized.

Self-ownership, the core of "one's own" or *suum* in Latin, is thus natural in sense 1, and one's own is the basis for liberty, in the main sense in which Smith uses the term. So liberty has a good claim to being natural in sense 1. Now, can liberty claim to be natural in senses 2, 3, and 4?

Is liberty, in Smith's time and ours, usual or expected? Yes and no. We will come back to the "yes" in our next essay, but here we highlight the "no." Arbitrary political arrangements that yield economic and religious monopolies, burdensome tax schemes and regulations, restrictions on the freedom of movement and expression are the norm. We might say that the *unnaturalness* of liberty is presupposed by Smith's entire project. Why write a book like *The Wealth of Nations* if one believes liberty to be a natural tendency in political affairs? (See Brubaker 2006, 332.)

In his *Lectures on Jurisprudence*, which crib extensively from Hume's *History of England*, Smith tells of political development in England—which he reckoned the most liberal polity. In France and Spain, "the absolute power of the sovereigns has continu'd ever since its establishment.... In England alone a different government has been established from the natural course of things" (LJ 265). Against the natural course of things, Smith says, England didn't develop a large standing army; without a standing force, the sovereign had to assemble Parliament to go to war. English Parliament —the Commons in particular—asserted itself against the crown, leading, after great convulsions, to the shoring up of institutions supportive of individual liberty: the limit of royal prerogative, the firming up of the rule of law, the regularization of legal practice. For Smith and Hume, the existence of liberty in Britain, such as it was, was not usual or particularly expected.

The same feeling of the unnaturalness of liberty (in sense 2) runs through WN. Consider, again: "All systems either of preference or of restraint, therefore, being thus completely taken away, the obvious and simple system of natural liberty establishes itself of its own accord" (WN 687.51). Natural liberty does not simply establish itself of its own accord. Systems of preference and restraint flow ubiquitously from aspects of human nature: partiality, desire for public esteem, limited knowledge, and so on. It is within Smith's contemplation and judgment that systems of preference and restraint are taken away. Only then, and within such a vision, does the system of natural liberty emerge as obvious and simple.[3]

Natural liberty is natural because it is worth naturalizing. The

3. This paragraph and the next draws from Brubaker (2006, 338).

system of natural liberty may be taken as "some general, and even systematical, idea of the perfection of policy and law" intended to direct "the views of the statesman" (TMS 234.18). Smith realizes that the expectation that liberty "should ever be entirely restored in Great Britain, is as absurd as to expect that an Oceana or Utopia should be established in it" (WN 471.43). But his work attempts to persuade British political practice into beliefs that will augment liberty. His posture is presumptively in favor of a policy reform that allows individuals greater degrees of freedom to pursue their interests, within the rules of justice, in their own way, although it is possible that Smith will make an exception to the general presumption.

A presumption of liberty is worth naturalizing because it serves the good of humankind. Smith's economic analysis illustrates how commerce facilitates "the co-operation...of great multitudes" (WN 26.2). But the benefits of the market process depend upon liberty, the "liberal and generous system" (WN 671.24), not the "illiberal and oppressive" measures of mercantilism (WN 584.50).

Degrees of flourishing require degrees of liberalness in government policy. That shows how liberty is necessary and therefore may be said to be natural in sense 3. Although it is not a usual and expected feature of human history, some degree of liberty is necessary for the flourishing states of affairs described in WN, such as the "higgling and bargaining" dynamics of the price system (WN 49.4).

"Let the same natural liberty of exercising what species of industry they please be restored to all his majesty's subjects" (WN 470.42). Smith believes that the liberty of each individual *ought* to be honored, even though it can never be held inviolate, a liberty corresponding to the conventions of self-ownership and property between jural equals in the individual's society. Smith believes that each *ought* to be dignified in liberty, the way of better living. Built on the natural property that each soul has in his or her person (sense 1), the goodness of liberty (sense 4) is the principal reason why natural liberty is natural.

We leave this essay with a plan to continue on "natural." The next will consider "natural" versus "conventional," and suggest a concept, *natural convention*, which combines nature and convention.

CHAPTER 13

Nature, Convention, and Natural Convention

By Daniel Klein and Erik Matson

In the previous chapter, we said that liberty is natural in important senses of the term. We also said that liberty is a flipside of commutative justice. (CJ = commutative justice.)

Given that Smith is closely associated with David Hume, one may ask: How does all the naturalness square with a famous statement in *A Treatise of Human Nature*? Hume said that a sense of CJ "is not deriv'd from nature, but arises artificially."

Smith's account of justice differs slightly from Hume's. He more emphasizes the role of resentment and regards "utility" as a matter of secondary importance. (We treat the matter in Matson, Doran, and Klein 2019.) But whatever the daylight between them, Hume's distinction between natural and artificial still helps us think about ways in which liberty is and isn't natural for Smith. If CJ is artificial, and "not deriv'd from nature," how can we lavish liberty with naturalness?

Some of the most important words in Hume and Smith are polysemes. A contrariety might arise because one sentence uses the polyseme in one sense while another uses it in another. Hume and Smith both played with *nature* and *natural*. Other polysemes include *reason, liberty*, and *convention* in Hume, and *justice* and *impartial spectator* in Smith.

Also, in 1775 Hume disavowed the *Treatise*, which was published in parts in 1739 and 1740. That doesn't mean that we should disregard what Hume called his "juvenile work," but it does mean that if a statement in the *Treatise* conflicts with his thought generally and does not find life in his subsequent writings, it is reasonable to consider whether it was an act of juvenile indiscretion. That applies here, for in his subsequent writings the only mention of CJ as artificial comes in a footnote in an appendix of Hume's enquiry on morals, a footnote that obliterates the claim (Hume 1998, 99).

Moreover, in the *Treatise* itself Hume walked back the notion that justice is not natural. He accords justice a place among the "laws of nature" because it is "obvious and absolutely" necessary for social life. "Hume's aim," Stephen Buckle (1991, 298) writes, "is not to replace natural law, but to complete it." In a similar vein Knud Haakonssen (1981, 12) writes that Hume combined "the strands of his inheritance into a completely new sort of natural law theory —for, indeed, he is quite willing to use that label, provided we let him fill in the contents himself."

What is Hume's "new sort of natural law theory"? The theory flows out of Hume's notion of convention, a word often set in opposition to nature. Expositing Humean convention helps us transcend the opposition and propose "natural convention." The idea of natural convention illumines liberty's naturalness.

There is no such thing as the only possible convention

It is a convention among English speakers to call the thing we normally sip coffee from a "cup." Meanwhile, among Swedes the convention is "kopp."

One of the key elements that make the regularity of saying "cup" a convention is that there is an alternative possible regularity, such as "kopp," which, too, would satisfy the other elements making a convention among English speakers. If "kopp" were the regularity among English speakers, some English speaker John would say "kopp," and he would want each of the other English speakers to say "kopp." As David K. Lewis (1969) put it, "there is no such thing as the only possible convention."

We could say "kopp," but we happen to say "cup." The important thing is that we are "on the same page"—that expression implies that there are other possible pages on which we could mutually coordinate. Thus, convention carries a connotation of the adventitious, inessential, or even arbitrary—"Which page shall we pick up at?" That which is conventional did not arise by necessity. It was not dictated by nature.

However, isn't it usual, expected, and beneficial, even necessary in some respects, that an American, among Americans, say "cup"? Isn't it *natural* for Americans to say "cup"?

Consider the following deeper regularity: *That one raised up in a language community, or long integrated into it, speak the language of that community.* Upon that deeper regularity it follows, given the semantics of the two languages, that Americans say "cup" and Swedes say "kopp."

Now, is that deeper regularity, too, a convention? No, it is not. There is not an alternative regularity that, too, would satisfy the other elements making convention. Indeed, it is unclear what that other regularity would even be. But if you imagine one, realize that it has to satisfy other conditions for convention, notably: under general adhesion to the regularity, John's conforming to it is good for John, and each other person's conforming to it is good for John. There is no such alternative regularity. Thus, we lack warrant for calling the deeper regularity conventional. Recall Lewis's words:

There is no such thing as the only possible convention. Hence, that deeper regularity is *not* a convention.

It is apt to call that deeper regularity natural. It is usual, expected, and beneficial, even necessary in some respects, on a wider plane of human experience. Underneath that which is conventional ("cup" rather than "kopp") we can often find a deeper and more abstract behavioral regularity, even spanning countries and epochs, that is not conventional but rather natural.

We said that in the *Treatise* Hume walked back CJ as artificial. Here is the most notable passage:

> To avoid giving offence [Ha!], I must here observe, that when I deny justice to be a natural virtue, I make use of the word, *natural*, only as oppos'd to *artificial*. In another sense of the word; as no principle of the human mind is more natural than a sense of virtue; so no virtue is more natural than justice. Mankind is an inventive species; and where an invention is obvious and absolutely necessary, it may as properly be said to be natural as any thing that proceeds immediately from original principles, without the intervention of thought or reflexion. Tho' the rules of justice be *artificial*, they are not *arbitrary*. Nor is the expression improper to call them *Laws of Nature*; if by natural we understand what is common to any species, or even if we confine it to mean what is inseparable from the species. (2007, 311)

In fact, winks of CJ as natural come in many spots in the wake of Hume's declaration that it is artificial. (See: "nature provides a remedy," "nature must furnish the materials," "this progress of sentiments be *natural*," "and also by the laws of nature," "invention of the law of nature," "three fundamental laws of nature," "observance of these rules follows *naturally*.") Remember what Hume's *Treatise* is a treatise of.

If, underneath the surface, the rules of CJ are natural, in what sense are they "artificial"? In what sense are they conventional?

CJ as conventional

The previous chapter said that, by the special knowledge and control that each soul has over its person, David Friedman (1994) proposed that your person is your "natural property," and we may add immediate possessions. And we said that would go even in the primeval state, and that Hume said as much in speaking of the special relation we have with our mind and body. Property implies ownership, a norm bearing on others not to mess.

For society to advance, objects not yet propertized in the primeval state need to be propertized. People, Hume said,

> must seek for a remedy, by putting these goods, as far as
> possible, on the same footing with the fix'd and constant
> advantages of the mind and body. This can be done after
> no other manner, than by a **convention** enter'd into by
> all the members of the society to bestow stability on the
> possession of those external goods, and leave every one
> in the peaceable enjoyment of what he may acquire by
> his fortune and industry. (Hume 2007, 314; emph. added)

Understand that "a convention enter'd into" does not imply contract. Hume immediately says: "This convention is not of the nature of a *promise*." Hume used the word *convention* in an innovative way that would eventually find definitive exposition in Lewis's book

Convention; A Philosophical Study (1969). We discuss Hume's innovation in "Convention without Convening" (Matson and Klein 2022).

Not everything that is agreeable arises from contractual agreement. A lovely spring day is agreeable, but did not arise from agreement. Likewise, when two men "pull the oars of a boat," they find a mutually coordinated pace "tho' they have never given promises to each other" (2007, 315). "In like manner are languages gradually establish'd by human conventions without any promise. In like manner do gold and silver become the common measures of exchange" (2007, 315).

By "artificial," Hume means post-primeval. He speaks of man "in *uncultivated nature*" and "in his rude and more *natural* condition." Note how those phrasings allow *cultivated* nature and man's *less-but-still* natural condition. Again, according to Hume and Smith, the basic principle of ownership gets *extended*. It is those extensions, beyond the primeval state, that Hume is calling artificial.

The basic precept of CJ is: Don't mess with other people's stuff. But what counts as "stuff"? Say it is England in the year 1400. And what makes the stuff one person's rather than another's, or no one's? And what counts as "messing with" it? Answers to those questions were filled in by particular rules operative in that time and place. Those rules—among jural equals—provided the social grammar of that time and place, just as Middle English provided a linguistic grammar. These answers were conventional, even if they bore close resemblance to conventions of other times or places. But conventions do change somewhat. Have you ever tried reading Middle English?

Consider testamentary succession in England in 1400. Suppose a family proposed to disregard entailments on its lands, which restrict to whom the property can pass. Would that be a violation of CJ? Would it be messing with someone's stuff? CJ rules as regards testamentary specifications have varied over time, with convention. For conventions as between two different contexts, it is sometimes foolish to think that one was right while the other was wrong, just as it would be foolish to say that Americans are right to say "cup" and Swedes wrong to say "kopp."

Or jump much further back in time, to 10,000 BC: Smith says that land itself was not propertized until the third stage of social development, agriculture. Whether what one did with land was in line with CJ would depend on certain conventions of time and place.

CJ as natural

We should understand CJ's basic precept—don't mess with other people's stuff—firstly as the jural relationship between jural equals, like you and your neighbor. It is a general principle, and many of its specifics must be filled in by the conventions of time and place. Systems of CJ vary somewhat by time and place.

But there is uniformity amidst variety. Whatever time and place we speak of, the society won't fare well if neighbors mess with each other's stuff. Smith said that a basic regard for CJ's precept is "indispensable." Hume said that without such regard "society must immediately dissolve." Thus, if we speak of society, there must be some basic regard for shared understandings of CJ. That uniformity spells natural: usual, expected, necessary for the state of social existence supposed in discourse, and beneficial. Even in the primeval state, fellow members of the Paleolithic band presumably did not much mess with one another's stuff.

CJ as natural convention

We can define natural convention as a social practice whose concrete form in time and place allows for various expressions (and is therefore conventional), but whose generalized form is necessary (and hence natural) to social development beyond the primeval state.

CJ is a prime example of a natural convention. Other examples include political authority and language. There are (and have been) myriad understandings of what, exactly, constitutes property and how that cashes out in social and legal practice. Those myriad understandings give rise to corresponding notions about property violations. But, throughout, is the idea that property is not to be violated; *in every community*, violations of property give rise to the passion of resentment. The community's manifestations of CJ are distinctive in many respects, and adherence to those conventions is mutually agreeable. But the general form of CJ, across communities, is natural. There is uniformity amidst variety.

In *The Fatal Conceit* (1988, 17), Friedrich Hayek provides an analogy: "There may exist just one way to satisfy certain requirements for forming an extended order—just as the development of wings is apparently the only way in which organisms can become able to fly (the wings of insects, birds, and bats have quite different genetic origins)." Wings are the only way for organisms to fly, even though in nature we see many different types of wings. So too are extended notions of CJ the only way for a society to advance beyond the primeval, even though we see different conventions of CJ.

Liberty as natural convention

In the previous chapter, we noted ways in which liberty is not usual or expected. Now, we highlight ways in which it is, and therefore in those senses natural.

Again, liberty, in the way that Smith's WN primarily uses the word, is a flipside of CJ, and CJ is necessary to any sustainable community. In a modern nation-state, neighbors generally refrain from messing with each other's stuff. As for the governor-governed jural relationship, the government institutionalizes its "messings" in the form of taxation and myriad restrictions.

In any time and place, CJ conceptually pins down the contours of liberty in that setting, on the following principle: *An action taken by government is an initiation of coercion if and only if such action if taken by a neighbor or other jural equal would be an initiation of coercion.*

Thus, as long as CJ is alive among neighbors, liberty naturally exists *as a concept.* Like CJ, the specific contours of liberty vary somewhat with time and place. But we can pin down those contours by consulting the conventions of CJ among jural equals in that time and place. Smith's expressions associated with liberty— for example, "of their own accord," "allowing every man to pursue his own interest his own way"—become substantively meaningful as pinned down by the principle stated in the preceding paragraph.

And liberty usually spells prosperity. Societies with liberal policies, therefore, grow rich and come to have outsized military, political, cultural, and economic influence. Thus, there is some basis to expect liberal tendencies. Something usual or expected is in that sense natural.

And, as we said previously, liberal policy is generally beneficial for the whole, and in that sense, too, natural. A presumption of liberty is worth naturalizing. It is proper to instill attachments to a presumption of liberty.

To sum up:

1. Liberty has a conceptual dual in CJ.

2. CJ begins, even in the primeval band, with the soul's ownership of its person, and history then extends the principle of ownership to other objects.

3. CJ is natural although particulars vary, as with wings among species of flying organisms.

4. As CJ is pinned down, substantively, in time and place, so too is liberty.

5. Liberty presents itself as a coherent principle of nature. Tyrants will battle against liberty but they cannot destroy it as a living idea without destroying society.

Liberal civilization, which is only several centuries old, is a newcomer to the pageant of human history. But the principles of individual self-ownership and equal, rule-of-law subjection under government, and a presumption of liberty bearing on government, can be called natural conventions—if only for the subpopulation cherishing those principles—of a natural development in the story of humankind.

CHAPTER 14

McCloskey's Narrative and Jurisprudence

D eirdre McCloskey awakens us to the Great Enrichment, which began a decade or two after *The Wealth of Nations* was published in 1776. Her bourgeois trilogy (McCloskey 2006; 2010; 2016) and other books (McCloskey 2019; McCloskey and Carden 2020) treat the causes. It is a story of growing openness during the 17th and 18th centuries to "having a go."

Liberal sentiments and ideas were communicated by speech and print. Persuasion and edification came by intellectual and moral leadership. The paramount figure was and is Adam Smith. He morally authorized your having a go, and morally authorized *allowing others* to have a go—liberalization. Adam Smith called it "allowing every man to pursue his own interest his own way" (WN 664.3). McCloskey's story is the lead-up to that cresting of cultural leadership and the resultant enrichment.

McCloskey's narrative is worth enhancing. I accentuate the role of jurisprudence, about which McCloskey says only a little. We can understand how crucial jurisprudence was historically only by understanding how crucial it is conceptually.

Ngrams bolster McCloskey's narrative

Below is a diagram of five ngrams—four 2grams and one 3gram. One of the 2grams is "virtuous industry," charted by the dark blue line. The vertical axis is the percentage of all gazillion 2grams in millions of books that are "virtuous industry."

The striking thing about the figure is the flatline from 1675 to about 1740 for most of the ngrams shown. "Virtuous industry" was zilch—zilch!—from 1675 to 1736, and then some people started writing "virtuous industry." Virtue + industry, what a notion!

FIG. 14.1: NGRAMS: "HONEST," ETC.

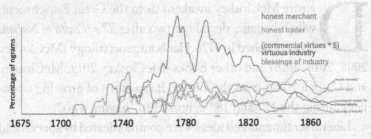

It's similar for "honest trader," "blessings of industry," "honest merchant," and "commercial virtues." The last one I've multiplied by 5 to make it visible with the others. All of the lines were zilch and then came into being. McCloskey says that commerce and industry became honored. Formerly regarded as lacking in virtue, commerce and industry became respectable, even virtuous. The lines beautifully illustrate what she says.

Likewise, "fair profits" and "honest profits" prove that McCloskey is right: Around 1770 some people started to talk of "fair profits" and "honest profits." Profits could be fair and honest—who knew?!

FIG. 14.2: NGRAMS: "FAIR" AND "HONEST" PROFITS

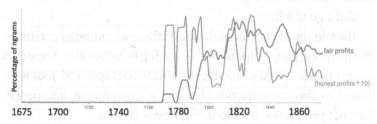

In *Bourgeois Equality* (2016, ch. 25), McCloskey says that the word *honest* underwent profound change. In Shakespeare's time, honest meant noble, aristocratic, loyal, honorable. By Smith's time, it had shifted to how we think of it—truthful, upright—and for all. McCloskey demonstrates the change, and that "an identical shift occurs in non-English Germanic languages" (2016, 247). To illustrate, she quotes TMS: "The poor man must neither defraud nor steal from the rich…. There is no commonly honest man who does not more dread the inward disgrace of such an action" (TMS 138.6). McCloskey writes: "In Shakespeare 'commonly honest' would commonly be an honest contradiction in terms and 'honest but poor' an absurdity" (2016, 240).

In the ngram figures above, look at the "honest" lines: Before the eighteenth century, "honest merchant," "honest trader," "honest profits" are zero. The figures confirm McCloskey's narrative.

After Adam Smith, Tocqueville's America of the 1830s largely subscribed to the new gospel: "In the United States professions are more less onerous, more or less lucrative, but they are never high or low. Every honest profession is honorable" (2000, 526).

Having a go—but at what?

McCloskey's story is about Smith and others morally authorizing your having a go, and morally deauthorizing your preventing others from having a go.

But a go at what?

Back in the old traditional society, there was more of a status or station in carving stone for hire or baking bread for sale. Vocations more often involved a sanctification and social approval. Jobs were boxed in also by restrictions backed by government, and people had not yet learned how to think outside the box.

With growing towns, trade, and the teachings of jurisprudence, a more abstract notion arose, a notion of honest dealings. It is as though cultural leaders began to say: We're learning that the world is too darned complicated to pretend to know, and we will pretend no longer to track the particulars of time and place. As long as you don't mess with anyone's stuff, have a go and we'll recognize the pecuniary residuals as fair profits. Earnings. Honest income.

But are people to win a livelihood at prostitution and salacious arts? And what about blasphemy? Sedition, treason, and pernicious moral and political literature?

Many a menace to liberal civilization got rich through the honest dealings involved in writing and publishing books. Having a go may be conducted to honest profit, but such profiting may not be virtuous. A tension surrounds the problem of profiting that is honest but not virtuous. That is but one of the quandaries of liberalism.

Fortunately, the arc of liberalism grappled with the paradoxes and continued upward. A key was to clarify honest as distinct from virtuous. Justice had layers. In equal-equal relationships, honest was, in effect, advanced as a necessary but not sufficient condition for virtuous (Klein 2019). A conceptualization of honest—or *just*, in a basic, mere sense, clarified by jural theorists—came forward. The conceptualization opened up new ways of seeing things, and sparked the imagination. People were allowed and even encouraged to think outside the box. The result was *innovation*, the electric spark in the engine of enrichment.

Consider the rise of "earnings" and "income":

FIGURE 14.3: NGRAMS: "INCOME," "EARNINGS"

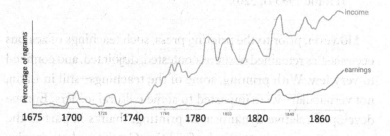

Both "earnings" and "income" pick up after 1740. Think about what "earnings" means. It means what you net from your honest commerce, whether you sell goods or services. Never mind what goods or services. It's really quite abstract. Earnings are what you have from your honest dealings, whatever those dealings might be.

Jurisprudence, the printing press, the vernacular, literacy, and press dynamism

Scholars like Brian Tierney have explained that notions of permissive, open-ended individual rights start up significantly in the 12th century, and a steady stream of those notions flows into the Dutchman Hugo Grotius. Moreover, the Romans had developed jurisprudence. In a sketch of European history, Hume wrote:

> [P]erhaps there was no event, which tended farther to
> the improvement of the age, than one, which has not
> been much remarked, the accidental finding of a copy
> of Justinian's Pandects, about the year 1130, in the town

of Amalfi in Italy. The ecclesiastics, who had leisure, and some inclination of study, immediately adopted with zeal this excellent system of jurisprudence, and spread the knowledge of it throughout every part of Europe (Hume 1983 II, 520).

However, prior to the printing press, such teachings of zealous ecclesiastics remained obscure, contested, disjointed, and confined to very few. With printing, some of the teachings—still in Latin, not vernacular—were imparted to some cultural leaders. Europe developed relative dynamism in printing, thanks in part to the continent's porous patchwork of polities. Grotius and others give a whole new momentum to jurisprudence.

Although Grotius did not invent jurisprudence when he published the three-volume *The Rights of War and Peace* in 1625, the publication was a major development. In 1839 Henry Hallam wrote: "It is acknowledged by every one, that the publication of this treatise made an epoch in the philosophical, and almost, we might say, the political history of Europe" (Hallam 1839, 181).

Spurred in part by the Protestant emphasis on a direct and personal connection with God and hence scripture, literacy was taking root. But it was slow to expand. Only in the vernacular and with rising print-culture could ideas be propounded to that emergent entity called "the people" or "the public."

When it came to works in jurisprudence, a Briton's ability to read English might not even be good enough, as in the earlier part of the eighteenth century, some of the important works were still composed in Latin, including ones by Glasgow professors Gershom Carmichael and Francis Hutcheson. In Britain, jurisprudence comes to be written and taught *in the English language* only in the eighteenth century. Thus, from 1675 to the 1740s, the English word *jurisprudence* was little used. Nonetheless, jurisprudential teachings were important for Latinate cultural leaders like Carmichael and Hutcheson.

But after 1740, with Latin waning, usage of the word *jurisprudence* rose steadily to about 1790, as the following figure shows.

FIG. 14.4: NGRAMS: "JURISPRUDENCE"

The chief jural idea that I wish to accentuate was a distinction between plain, honest dealings and other, fuzzier ethical duties. Plain, honest dealings were voluntary interactions, with no messing with other people's stuff. If you made money from honest dealings, the result was earnings.

Jurisprudence schooled Europe in a social grammar

Nowadays, an unspecified dirty word is called an expletive, but originally "expletive" meant an unspecified word in a grammatical construction. That might be why Grotius (2005, 142-47, 951-55) called the grammar-like sense of justice *expletive justice*. It connoted grammar, in particular the relationship between parts of the sentence. Adam Smith and others called that justice commutative justice. It, too, connotes part-to-part, just as a commuter travels point-to-point. Part-to-part stands in contradistinction to whole-to-part or part-to-whole.

"The most sacred laws" of commutative justice, Smith said, guard your neighbor's person, property, and promises-due (TMS, 84.2). The rules of its precept are "precise and accurate," or grammar-like. The precept of commutative justice provides a social grammar.

I say "precept" to abstract away from what happens once the precept is violated; jurisprudence thusly distinguished between a law's *precept* and its *sanction*. Once messing starts, things of course remain somewhat messy, no matter how thoroughly the law tries to specify sanctions by details of the case. It is the precept, not the sanctions, that Smith touts as "precise and accurate."

The rules of the precept evolved with society, and evolved to be precise and accurate. They were not invented by jural theorists, just as grammar was not invented by grammarians. Sometimes rules remain tacit until theorists study them. Smith said that often the precept of a rule prescribes "no more than common sense dictates to any man tho' he had never heard there was such a rule" (LRBL 73). The time-and-place rules of commutative justice are a prime example of natural convention (see chapter 13).

But jural theory did have consequences. The analysis and articulation of customary rules of commutative justice by men like Grotius clarified what counts as honest dealings, for example by analyzing the nature of consent and contract in various circumstances. It considered the sources of ownership. During the Thirty Years War, objects came into people's possession in odd ways: Were they legitimately owned by the current possessor? And what about reputation (Bonica and Klein 2021)? Is it covered by commutative justice? Jural theory formulated and clarified what it meant to mess with your neighbor's stuff. It thereby instructed one on what *not* to do.

For equal-equal jural relationships, the drift was, to use the analogy of rules for writing: Write whatever sentences your imagination conjures, but do not violate grammar. With commutative justice pinned down in a time and place, this message was often accompanied by tactful counsel for the jural superior, that is, the rulers or governors: Maybe you should try to abstain from actions which if they were done by an equal in equal-equal relationships would be regarded as criminal. Thus, jurisprudence gave wings to policy precepts that would, beginning in the 1770s, come to be called "liberal."

Jurisprudence kindled focalism and innovism

Let us return to McCloskey's narrative about economic activity. The clarification of commutative justice opened up the hyperspace of having a go—an honest go. Again, not all of it was ethical or virtuous—just as one may write a vicious yet grammatically correct sentence. But a certain presumption was given to honest income, while reservations and exceptions would be matters for the two looser conceptions of justice.

It broke "having a go" wide open. It wasn't just the traditional vocations of carving stone or baking bread. It was *anything you could imagine.* Thus, two things were happening simultaneously: (1) jural theorists were clarifying the category of honest income, and (2) moral leaders were authorizing the pursuit of honest income.

Honest income is but a part of the individual's local interests. Being more concrete, local interests make for focal points in everyday life. They are matters we can advance effectively, because they are matters of which we have some knowledge and influence. The moral authorization given to focal interests is what Erik Matson calls *focalism* (2022a). Focalism is the moral endorsement of focusing on one's local good, within moral constraints, beginning with those clarified by jural theory. Within such moral constraints, focalist efforts generally conduce to the good of the whole. Here we have the spontaneous-order meaning of "invisible hand."

The moral authorization of focalism and the conceptual openness of honest income invigorated enterprise like never before. Enterprise and honest innovation became God's work. McCloskey calls the surge *innovism*: "the frenetic bettering of machines and procedures and institutions after 1800, supported by a startling change in the ethical evaluation of the betterings" (McCloskey 2016, 93). Adam Smith quietly urged innovation and dynamism in calling for reform "where every man was *perfectly free* both to chuse what occupation he thought proper, and *to change it as often as he thought proper*" (WN 116, italics added).

Jurisprudence begot liberalism and liberal political economy

Smith's younger associate Dugald Stewart wrote that systems of natural jurisprudence provided "the first rudiments…of liberal politics taught in modern times" (Stewart 1854, 26, cf. 183). We needed jurisprudence to clarify the abstract category of honest dealings or earnings, which would then be morally authorized, and then be advanced in policy reform, all leading to innovism. We needed jurisprudence to clarify liberty—the government not messing with one's stuff. J. G. A. Pocock says it succinctly: "the child of jurisprudence is liberalism" (Pocock 1983, 249).

Stewart wrote that it is also to jurisprudence that "we are chiefly indebted for the modern science of Political Economy" (Stewart 1854, 171). The very concepts of "the free market" and "intervention" are rooted in the formulations of commutative justice: not messing with other people's stuff. Jurisprudence was critical to the development of economic thought. The figure below indicates a sharp rise in economic discourse in the 1740s and 1750s.

FIG. 14.5: NGRAMS: "COMMERCE," ETC.

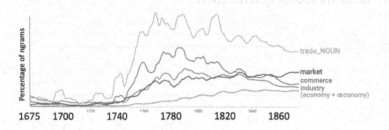

Liberal heart and liberal spine

Deirdre McCloskey rightly tells us that ideas matter, talk matters, culture matters, moral authorization matters, moral leadership matters. That is how the world works. The evidence of ngrams bolsters her theory.

But what is the good? McCloskey's answer is liberal civilization. A leader for our time, she tells us to cherish it and to identify with it.

The role of jural theory, both historically and conceptually, in the making of the Great Enrichment, though once better understood, fell into neglect. Perhaps it did so because it presents paradoxes and it embarrasses slogans, denials, and taboos (Diesel and Klein 2021). Whatever the reasons for its neglect, the jural theory of Grotius and others clarified and still clarifies the liberty that is at the center of what Smith called "the liberal plan" (WN 664.3). Benjamin Constant would associate it with "modern liberty" and Isaiah Berlin with "negative liberty" (see ch. 17). The liberty maxim is the spine of liberal civilization, and we must grapple amicably with the difficulties if we are to maintain and strengthen that spine.

The spine depends on heart. Our future turns on love. The grave menace is the governmentalization of social affairs. We must stand up to ideas and activities which tend toward that evil. The health of the spine begins in the chest.

CHAPTER 15

Moral Sentiment, Passive and Active, and Liberalism

Though not made explicitly, a distinction emerges in Adam Smith's *The Theory of Moral Sentiments* between passive moral sentiments, aptly called *emotions*, and active moral sentiments, aptly called *passions*. Such a distinction follows Lord Kames (1762, 37): "An internal motion or agitation of the mind, when it passeth away without desire, is denominated *an emotion*: when desire follows, the motion or agitation is denominated *a passion*."

A taxonomy of other-directed moral sentiments

Mary regards Jim's conduct and develops sentiments about its propriety or beauty. Sentiments about another's conduct or character are *moral* sentiments.

An active sentiment, or passion, is one that motivates. Mary feels a passion if she regards Jim's conduct and the resultant moral sentiments motivates her toward some action. The action might be other-directed, but that "other" might be someone other than Jim: For example, it might be Jim's benefactor or Jim's tormenter. The other-directed passions most central to Smith's analysis are gratitude and resentment. Gratitude is a positive passion, motivating recompense. Resentment is a negative passion, motivating punishment or retaliation.

A passive sentiment, or emotion, is more about one's disposition and emotional reaction upon receiving information or thoughts about the person liked or disliked, and doesn't necessarily motivate action. The other-directed passive sentiments or emotions most central in the book are, on the positive side, liking and love, and, on the negative side, disliking and hatred.

FIG. 15.1: MORAL SENTIMENTS, PASSIVE AND ACTIVE

	MORAL SENTIMENTS			
	passive	*active*		
	EMOTIONS	PASSIONS Passions tend to be reciprocating:		
Positive	liking, love	gratitude	recompensing, remunerating, reward	
Negative	disliking, hatred	resentment	retaliating, redressing, rectifying	

Two thought experiments

Adam Smith posed two pinky-earthquake thought experiments —the bracketed words in boldface are my insertions:

> [**Thought experiment 1: passive:**] Let us suppose that the great empire of China, with all its myriads of inhabitants, was suddenly swallowed up by an earthquake, and let us consider how a man of humanity in Europe, who had no sort of connexion with that part of the world, would be affected upon receiving intelligence of this dreadful calamity. He would, I imagine, first of all,

express very strongly his sorrow for the misfortune of that unhappy people, he would make many melancholy reflections upon the precariousness of human life, and the vanity of all the labours of man, which could thus be annihilated in a moment. He would too, perhaps, if he was a man of speculation, enter into many reasonings concerning the effects which this disaster might produce upon the commerce of Europe, and the trade and business of the world in general. And when all this fine philosophy was over, when all these humane sentiments had been once fairly expressed, he would pursue his business or his pleasure, take his repose or his diversion, with the same ease and tranquillity, as if no such accident had happened. The most frivolous disaster which could befal himself would occasion a more real disturbance. If he was to lose his little finger to-morrow, he would not sleep to-night; but, provided he never saw them, he will snore with the most profound security over the ruin of a hundred millions of his brethren, and the destruction of that immense multitude seems plainly an object less interesting to him, than this paltry misfortune of his own. [**Thought experiment 2: active:**] To prevent, therefore, this paltry misfortune to himself, would a man of humanity be willing to sacrifice the lives of a hundred millions of his brethren, provided he had never seen them? Human nature startles with horror at the thought, and the world, in its greatest depravity and corruption, never produced such a villain as could be capable of entertaining it. [**Questions about the two thought experiments:**] But what makes this difference? When our passive feelings are almost always so sordid

and so selfish, how comes it that our active principles
should often be so generous and so noble? When we are
always so much more deeply affected by whatever concerns ourselves, than by whatever concerns other men;
what is it which prompts the generous, upon all occasions, and the mean upon many, to sacrifice their own
interests to the greater interests of others? (TMS 136-7)

The two thought experiments draw the contrast between passive and active. Our passive sentiments are "almost always so sordid and so selfish," whereas our active sentiments are more often
"so generous and so noble." Thus, in the passive thought experiment, the pinky looms larger, whereas in the active the earthquake
looms larger.

The passivity of rooting for your team, voting, and being governed

I see party politics as more about passive sentiments, emotion, rather than active sentiment or passion. That is, partisanship is more
about liking and disliking.

As Paul Simon put it in "Mrs. Robinson":

Sitting on a sofa on a Sunday afternoon

Going to the candidates' debate

Laugh about it, shout about it

When you've got to choose

Every way you look at this you lose

What liberalism understands

The governmentalization of social affairs throws us into the passive position. That is what liberalism understands.

CHAPTER 16

The Liberal Christening

I n the 1770s, Adam Smith and others affixed a political meaning to the word "liberal." In doing so, they christened their
political persuasion "liberal."

**FIG. 16.1: NGRAMS: "LIBERAL POLICY," "LIBERAL PRINCIPLES," "LIBERAL
IDEAS," "LIBERAL PLAN," "LIBERAL SYSTEM"**

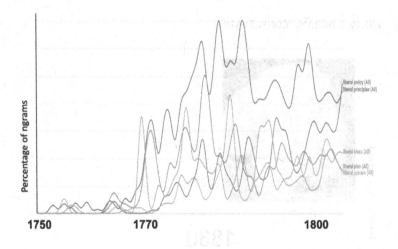

In Figure 16.1, each of the five ngrams consists of two words and
hence is a 2gram. The vertical axis is the percentage of all 2grams
in millions of books. (Access sources and data from links in the
original of this chapter at Svensktidskrift.se.)

The policy presumption of "allowing every man to pursue his

own interest his own way" was christened "liberal." The blossoming of Figure 16.1 gave rise to the term "liberalism." The first political liberalism was Smithian liberalism. It was a posture against the governmentalization of social affairs.

Some people have suggested that liberalism didn't exist before the word *liberalism*—that is, the noun ending in *-ism*—was used. As Shakespeare pointed out, roses smell sweet irrespective of what we call them. Roses existed before English speakers used "rose." Rocks existed before English speakers used the word "rocks." The sun existed before English speakers used the word "sun"—long before.

Likewise, Samuel Johnson and conservatism existed before 1830:

FIG. 16.2: NGRAM: "CONSERVATISM"

Anthony Benezet and abolitionism existed before 1830.

FIG. 16.3: NGRAM: "ABOLITIONISM"

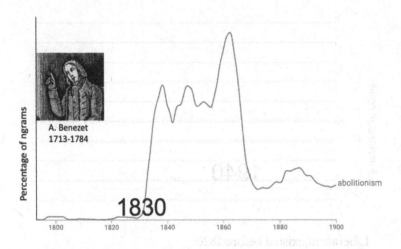

Protectionism existed long before 1860:

FIG. 16.4: NGRAM: "PROTECTIONISM"

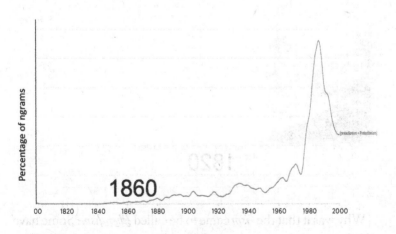

Racism and sexism existed long before the 1930s:

FIG. 16.5: NGRAMS: "RACISM," "SEXISM"

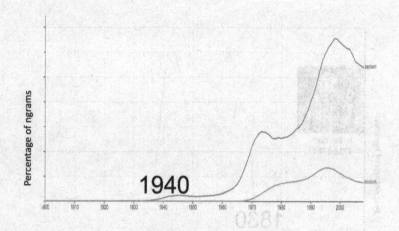

Liberalism existed before 1820:

FIG. 16.6: NGRAMS: "LIBERALISM" (WITH AND WITHOUT THE L CAPITALIZED)

Why was it that the *-ism* came to be called *liberalism*? Some have said that a political meaning of "liberal" started on the Continent and that Britain imported it from the Continent. People talk about the Spanish *Liberales* circa 1810. Among those who have said that Britain imported the term "liberal" in a political sense from the Continent are Helena Rosenblatt (2018, 42), Jörn Leonhard (2004), Daisy Hay (2008, 310, 312), David M. Craig (2012, 469, 481ff.), R. R. Palmer and Joel Colton (2007, 428), J. Salwyn Shapiro (1958, 9), Auguste Nefftzer (1883), James Fitzjames Stephen (1862), and an anonymous writer in the Tory journal *Blackwood's* in 1823.

Hayek in his day heard such rumors, but thought differently:

> It is often suggested that the term "liberal" derives from the early nineteenth-century Spanish party of the *liberales*. I am more inclined to believe that it derives from the use of the term by Adam Smith in such passages as *W.o.N.*, II, 41: "the liberal system of free exportation and free importation" and p. 216: "allowing every man to pursue his own interest his own way, upon the liberal plan of equality, liberty, and justice. (Hayek 1960, 530 n13)

Now it's proven that Hayek was right and the others wrong. There is a lot of talk about how "big data" is going to make miracles and answer big questions. But when a great deal of interpretation and judgment is involved in utilizing the data, the touting of "big data" is hooey. Expect bias, don't believe big-data magic.

When interpretation and judgment are simple and straightforward, however, big data are powerful. The Google Ngram Viewer is simply counting and percentages. The data speak for themselves.

The most important figure in this chapter is Figure 16.1 because it shows the unmistakable and the original burgeoning of political "liberal" 2grams. To check that people didn't just start throwing "liberal" into all their 2gram collocations, Will Fleming made the analysis in Figure 16.7 for me. It shows, for example, that whereas "liberal policy" had been zero percent of all "liberal [noun]" expressions before 1770, in decades after 1770 it was between 1.5 and 3 percent of all such expressions.

FIG. 16.7: PERCENTAGE OF POLITICAL COLLOCATING NOUNS OUT OF TOP 100 COLLOCATING NOUNS, BY DECADE

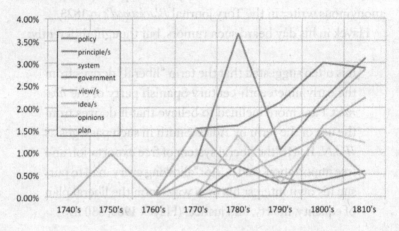

Figure 16.7 shows that the political expressions of "liberal" gained enormously (relative to their standing prior to 1770) among all "liberal [noun]" expressions. Again, it wasn't as though people just started adding the adjective "liberal" to their nouns. What you see in Figure 16.1 is real; it means exactly what your first impression suggests it means.

Next, Ben Bursae and I looked at all the pertinent authors—73, to be exact—at Liberty Fund's Online Library of Liberty, and that too confirms that, other than a couple of suggestive instances in David Hume (treated by Erik Matson 2022b), there's almost no sign of attaching a political meaning to "liberal" before 1769, the year of William Robertson's work *History of the Reign of Charles V*, which really kicks off the "liberal" christening.

Numerous other methods confirm that Hayek was right and the others wrong. British officialdom starts talking "liberal" in the Smithian fashion in the 1770s. For example, King George III used "liberal principles" in 1782 in a speech opening a session of Parliament. But, again, there are more data—simple counting—available. Todd Peckarsky and I coded all of the "liberal" and "illiberal" talk in 36 volumes of *The Parliamentary History of England* to the year 1803. Again, the timing fits perfectly (the vertical axis is the absolute number of occurrences of "liberal"/"illiberal").

FIG. 16.8: NGRAM: "LIBERAL" IN BRITISH PARLIAMENTARY DEBATE, 1750–1803

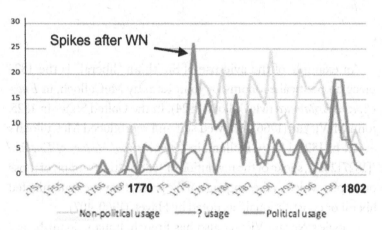

Then there is the leading liberal journal, *The Edinburgh Review*, which started up in 1802. Shanelka Payoe, Eric Hammer, and I coded "liberal" occurrences. Figure 16.9 shows two series. The lesser is the unambiguously political "liberal" and the greater adds in occurrences marked as perhaps political, showing a steady stream of Smithian "liberal."

FIG. 16.9: NGRAMS: *EDINBURGH REVIEW*, POLITICAL "LIBERAL," 1802-1824

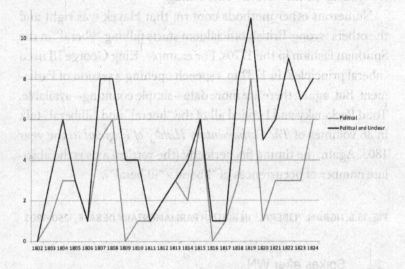

An example of the avid use of Smithian "liberal" is the 1824 piece on political economy by John Ramsay McCulloch, in *Encyclopedia Britannica* (McCulloch 1824). In the United States in 1825, John McVickar (1966) followed suit and reproduced McCulloch's essay. In 1827, Henry Hallam, in *Constitutional History of England* ([1827]2011), spoke of the revolution of 1688 as "the triumph of those principles which in the language of the present day are denominated liberal or constitutional," as noted by Hayek (1960, 407).

Google's Ngram Viewer also has French, Italian, Spanish, and German. Britain exported the "liberal" expressions of the Smithians to the Continent. The expressions in English, "liberal policy," etc., came to the French, Italian, Spanish, and German, but 20-plus years after they had already started up in English. Figure 16.10 shows it plainly—the panels are small but 1790 is marked clearly in each panel. (To see the details better, click the four links at the Svensktidskrift.se 2022 version of this piece.)

FIG. 16.10: FRENCH, ITALIAN, SPANISH, AND GERMAN FOR "LIBERAL" EXPRESSIONS, 1755–1830

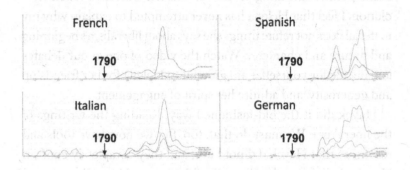

So now we know why the *-ism* that came along in the 1820s was "*liberal*ism." Once "liberalism" came along, it mopped up the 2gram expressions that had been used to signify Smithian liberalism:

FIG. 16.11: NGRAMS: "LIBERALISM" PARTLY DISPLACES THE EARLIER "LIBERAL" 2GRAMS.

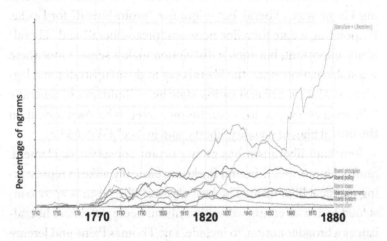

Helena Rosenblatt, author of the important 2018 book *The Lost*

History of Liberalism, and I have debated the matter on several occasions. Despite differences, we have become friends. Helena argues that a political meaning of "liberal" started with the French Revolution. I feel that Helena has never attempted to explain why my material does not refute things she says about liberalism's beginning and nature and character. Watch the video of one of our debates and decide for yourself. I am grateful to Helena for her friendship and generosity, and admire her spirit of engagement.

Hayek did it the old-fashioned way: Reading the writings of the liberal era. We must do that, too. But we now have tools and resources that Hayek did not have, and they completely confirm Hayek's belief that the "liberal" of the original liberalism started in Britain in the 1770s. For a decade I have been showing this evidence, and no one has ever challenged the evidence.

So, "liberal" in a political sense started up in the 1770s. How long before 1770 did liberalism exist? I think of Montaigne and Grotius as proto-liberals. It makes sense to see liberalism as tending to presuppose a stable, functional nation-state. I am comfortable saying Hume was a liberal, but might use "proto-liberal" for Locke. Pinpointing a date for a line between "proto-liberal" and "liberal" is not important, but such a distinction makes sense. Once there is a stable nation-state, the liberals say to the magistrates and legislators: Make it a liberal nation-state by, as Smith put it, generally "allowing every man to pursue his own interest his own way, upon the liberal plan of equality, liberty, and justice" (WN 664.3).

Smithian liberalism has an important conservative element. Smith, Hume, and Edmund Burke are basically alike in representing classical liberalism. The best classical liberalism is aptly construed today as conservative liberalism. Seeing classical liberalism as a broader notion, to include, say, Thomas Paine and Jeremy Bentham, is fair enough. I just think they represent inferior sorts of classical liberalism. Of the nineteenth century, Erik Gustaf Geijer and Alexis de Tocqueville are among those who best participate in the wisdom of Hume, Smith, and Burke.

Some call Hume racist. Kendra Asher (2022) explains that we should not read his infamous footnote shallowly.

A lot turned bad at the end of the nineteenth century. The Liberal Party in the United Kingdom changed its character and a new political meaning began to be attached to the word "liberal." We see in Figure 16.12 that from 1880 people started resorting to "new liberalism" and "old liberalism" to clarify what they meant.

FIG. 16.12: NGRAMS: "NEW LIBERALISM" AND ("OLD LIBERALISM" X 3)

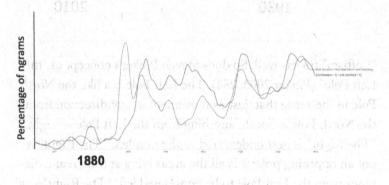

Bad semantics advanced from 1880. In the United States, the corruption of "liberal" started in the early twentieth century ("the progressive era"), but picked up under Franklin D. Roosevelt. North America especially, but the world has been stuck in the ruts, semantically. It is time to get out.

"Leftism" is a good name for leftism. In English, "leftist" and "left-wing" begin in the 1930s. Claims about "right" and "left" dating back to the French Revolution are overblown, even in the

French language. The term "progressive" is apt enough in the United States, but it is parochial to the United States. For a long time, American leftists have been bashful about admitting their leftism.

FIG. 16.13: NGRAMS: "LEFTIST," "LEFT-WING," "THE POLITICAL LEFT"

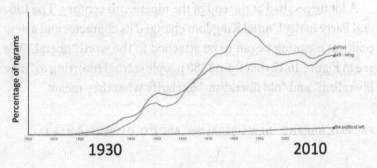

"Leftism" travels well. So does Steven Pinker's concept of "the Left Pole" (Pinker 2002, 284). The Left Pole is a like the North Pole in the sense that, just as movement in any direction from the North Pole is South, anything from the Left Pole is "right." "The Right" is best understood as the non-left. "The Right" is not an opposing pole; it is all the areas lying at too great a distance from the Left Pole to be considered left. "The Right"—or, non-left—is more diverse than the left. The non-left is coalitional first, and fusionist only sometimes. I like fusionism, but coalitionalism is more important. In his book *The Right*, Matthew Continetti (2022) quotes Russell Kirk saying in 1958 that all that can be reasonably hoped for "is a series of leagues and coalitions of anti-collectivist elements against the collectivist tendency of the times."

CHAPTER 17

The Recovery of Liberty

"Every one of these fundamental principles that have given us life, liberty, and prosperity is under attack," says Mark Levin in a television appearance.

Can the attack on liberty be turned back? Can we recover liberty?

To do that, we must advance a vital meaning of the word *liberty*. There is no question about it: We must go back, to go forward.

The vital meaning of liberty is the classical-liberal meaning. We must stick up for that meaning.

But it is not the only meaning, and we should not try to make it the only meaning. The classical-liberal meaning is vital—but it sits within an array of meanings, none to be despised.

An enumeration is provided by Raymond Aron, a great conservative liberal of France, who was born in 1905 and died in 1983. He enumerated four meanings (1994), listed here:

FIG. 17.1: FOUR MEANINGS OF *LIBERTY*

Raymond Aron	Benjamin Constant	Isaiah Berlin
Classical liberal meaning	"modern"	"negative" if given added specifications
Political participation	"ancient"	
National sovereignty		
Capabilities		"positive"

Also shown are the correspondences to Benjamin Constant's distinction between "modern" liberty and "ancient" liberty and to Isaiah Berlin's distinction between "negative" liberty and "positive" liberty.

The second meaning on Aron's list is political participation, associated with republicanism or democracy, especially direct and extensive participation. This meaning corresponds to Constant's ancient liberty. Ancient liberty, Constant (1819) said, "consisted in exercising collectively, but directly, several parts of the complete sovereignty; in deliberating, in the public square, over war and peace; in forming alliances with foreign governments; in voting laws, in pronouncing judgments; in examining the accounts, the acts, the stewardship of the magistrates; in calling them to appear in front of the assembled people, in accusing, condemning or absolving them."

The third meaning is national sovereignty, and hence not suzerainty or domination by a foreign state or power. This meaning looms large in issues of imperial powers and emergent secessionist movements.

The fourth meaning involves notions of enlarged capabilities: Winning the lottery augments your liberty. But the more important connection is to Berlin's positive liberty, where political quasi-religions have told people about how their true selves or potentialities would be liberated by grandiose political movements. Berlin (1969) told us to beware of positive liberty. He said: "historically more damage has been done by pseudo-positive than pseudo-negative liberty," and "positive liberty has been distorted more disastrously than negative liberty."

A classical liberal meaning of liberty

The classical liberal meaning of liberty starts with the virtue of commutative justice, which Adam Smith expressed as the duty of "abstaining from what is another's." *What is another's*, or one's own, was expressed in Latin as *suum*. For a classical liberal meaning of liberty, one's own or *suum* is understood in a narrow or grammar-like way. This *suum* may be summarized as person, property, and promises-due.

Suum or one's own (or one's "stuff") is delineated according to the rules of ownership of property and consent that operate among jural equals in the time and place of the society in question. Such rules may be said to be that society's most basic social grammar. Those rules constitute the individual's dominion that others are presumptively not to mess with.

Suppose your neighbor forcibly asserts that he is to get 35 percent of your income, or tells you that you are not to employ people for less than a certain wage. We'd consider such a neighbor to be initiating coercions. Classical liberals say it's coercion when done by government, too. Yes, government is a special sort of player in society. Its initiations of coercion are overt, institutionalized, openly rationalized. They are called intervention or restriction or regulation or taxation, rather than extortion, assault, theft, or trespass. But classical liberals maintain that they are initiations of coercion. Recognizing that helps to sustain a presumption against government coercions.

Whereas commutative justice is the duty of not messing with other people's stuff, *liberty* is others not messing with your stuff, particularly the government not messing with your stuff. In affirming this elemental concept of liberty, however, classical liberals do not equate liberty and the good.

The liberty maxim says: *By and large, in a choice between two reform options (one of which may be not to reform the status quo at all), the greater-liberty option is more desirable.*

Notice the "By and large." It is a maxim. When sustained within the culture, it expresses a presumption of liberty. But a presumption is defeasible. We maintain a presumption of innocence, but sometimes the defendant's innocence is *not* sustained.

The liberty maxim is formulated in terms of reforms. A reform implies a status quo. A status quo implies a society in time and place. From that status quo, the liberty maxim is directional, as opposed to destinational (Munger 2018). A classical liberal meaning of liberty need not be concerned with delineating "the free society" or "the proper role" of government. The contours of liberty may be grammar-like, but classical liberal claims for liberty are not grammar-like. They are loose, vague, and indeterminate, and they are circumstanced.

Classical liberals recognize that sometimes liberty must be sacrificed for the sake of liberty. A policy that reduces liberty directly might augment liberty overall (Klein and Clark 2010). Areas of contention include immigration, foreign policy, weapons policy, pollution, and financial doings for which the taxpayer is on the hook.

The liberty principle has its holes, gray areas, and exceptions; it does not speak to all important issues of government; and it is not self-justifying. Nonetheless, it remains cogent and gives a conceptual spine to classical liberalism. The liberty maxim—that the more-liberty option is presumptively the more desirable option—gives structure to the formulation of issues and positions on issues. We can argue over how strong the presumption is, and how it must compromise sometimes with another important presumption, namely, that of the status quo. But the liberty maxim remains the spine of classical liberalism.

Standing up for a meaning of a word

The spine of classical liberalism can be stiffened by Raymond Aron's list of meanings of liberty. That spine is fortified by seeing how a classical liberal meaning stands in relation to the others. Then we can focus on one at a time, and speak clearly of the vital importance of the classical liberal meaning.

The attack on that liberty is unrelenting. To get attackers to relent, it helps to clarify liberty. We are then in a better position to awaken them to the damage they do.

CHAPTER 18

When Diktats and Conscience Conflict

"It is beyond controversy among all good men," wrote Hugo Grotius in 1625, "that if the persons in authority command any thing contrary to Natural Law or the Divine Precepts, it is not to be done" (2011, 54).

Grotius was a Dutchman, and he knew something about bad laws. He once escaped imprisonment by hiding in a chest of books, and then wrote some of his works in exile.

I recently flew from Europe to the United States, and found that the mask mandate on the plane was often disregarded and rather laxly enforced by the staff. Everyone on the plane had just had a negative Covid test, many had had Covid, many (including me) had been vaccinated, many were not old or vulnerable. And besides, the communication of knowledge of effective treatments has reduced many hazards. In the minds of many, the mandate was inhumane and absurd.

Making children wear masks is, in my judgment, particularly awful and senseless. Likewise, vaccine mandates. If you agree and are in a position of having to carry out such orders, should you do so?

Hugo Grotius addressed the morality of enforcing bad laws. I quote his three-volume work, *The Rights of War and Peace*, a landmark in natural law or what was later called natural jurisprudence. Henry Hallam wrote in 1839, "It is acknowledged by every one,

that the publication of this treatise made an epoch in the philosophical, and almost, we might say, the political history of Europe"
(1839, III, 385). It is difficult to overstate the part Grotius played in
the emergence of liberal civilization. Here I quote Grotius's great
work as abridged and translated by William Whewell, published
in 1853 and reprinted in 2011.

The Rights of War and Peace defines war very broadly, to include
any sort of force or injury, even as may occur in a robbery. Because
Grotius first had to define "injury," he elaborated the operating
system, you might say, of basic justice—the grammar-like rules of
abstaining from what is another's. He then explores the constraints
that morality, or natural law, places on our conduct, once force or
injury has occurred.

Enforcing a bad law can be rather like visiting injury upon another and is like being commanded to wage unjust war. I realize that
it's a long way from enforcing mask and vaccine mandates to wag-
ing unjust war, but the principle is the same. Grotius (2011, 292)
quotes Tertullian:

> The law may not be content with its own conscience; it
> owes a justification to those for whom it claims obedi-
> ence. (Have lockdowns and mandates made any sense?)

> A law is suspected, which does not seek moral appro-
> bation. (The style of the Covidcrats is dictatorial and
> despotic.)

> A citizen does not obey the laws faithfully if he be igno-
> rant at what crime the punishment of the law is aimed.
> (What crime has the previously infected young person,
> for example, committed?)

Grotius (2011, 293) suggests that a hangman ought not carry out orders if he doubts the guilt of the person to be hanged: "It is also a probable opinion that an executioner who is to put a man to death, ought to know that there is a cause in his deserts for doing so; either as having been aware of the trial and proofs, or by the confession of the criminal."

Of those commanded to carry out injury upon innocents, he says:

> [I]f they are commanded to join in a war, as often happens, if they are quite clear that the war is unlawful, they ought to abstain. That God is to be obeyed rather than men, not only the Apostles have said, but Socrates also: and the masters among the Hebrews have a saying indicating that even the king, if he command anything against the law of God, is not to be obeyed. (Grotius 2011, 290)

Grotius by no means approved of rash disobedience of any law with which you happen to disagree. But you remain responsible to refrain from carrying out orders that your cool conscience tells you are absurd, violative of human dignity, and harmful to the common good.

Grotius taught European rulers their accountability to their subjects, to God, and to nature. He taught that the individual human being, as such, has natural rights. He taught rulers, through conscience and justice, to moderate their rule and their conflicts. There is a direct line from Grotius to Adam Smith's "liberal plan of equality, liberty, and justice" and to what Deirdre McCloskey calls the Great Enrichment.

Grotius is a great liberal because he sees that everyone has moral agency as an individual: Rulers are to be judged by the ruled. Everyone has the capacity and the responsibility to judge. Even in war, he suggests that all declarations of war be "accompanied by a declaration of the cause of the war; that the whole human race, as it were, might judge of its justice." Citing Aristotle, he insists, "justice is a virtue which belongs to man as man" (Grotius 2011, 292–93).

We are not slavish tools of autocrats or government agencies. "Stratocles was laughed at in Athens for proposing a law that whatever was thought good by Demetrius, should be reckoned right and pious" (Grotius 2011, 290). We laugh at YouTube, Facebook, and Twitter (pre-Musk, anyway) for shutting down discourse that challenges whatever they pretend to regard as the Mount Olympus of Covid wisdom.

Grotius (291) writes: "As in the proverb, and in Homer, *The day that makes man a slave takes half his worth away.*"

CHAPTER 19

Corruption according to Adam Smith

That awful person! How can someone be so corrupt?!

Be it a Hillary Clinton, Donald Trump, or someone else, Adam Smith pointed to an answer: "This self-deceit, this fatal weakness of mankind, is the source of half the disorders of human life" (TMS 158.6).

In the same work, *The Theory of Moral Sentiments,* Smith points to another source of corruption: "Of all the corrupters of moral sentiments, therefore, faction and fanaticism have always been by far the greatest" (TMS* 156.43).[1]

So, faction and fanaticism are the greatest corrupters of moral sentiments, and self-deceit is the source of half of the disorders of human life. Sounds like those sources must pretty well cover it.

Related to faction and fanaticism, Smith also says: "False notions of religion are almost the only causes which can occasion any very gross perversion of our natural sentiments in this way; and that principle which gives the greatest authority to the rules of duty, is alone capable of distorting our ideas of them in any considerable degree" (TMS 176.12).

But wait! Smith writes: "The great source of both the misery and disorders of human life, seems to arise from over-rating the difference between one permanent situation and another" (TMS* 149.31).

1. In this chapter, the * in citations indicates that the quotation *was new to Ed 6 of 1790.*

Seems he has surpassed the ceiling of 100 percent.

And there's more. Smith speaks of burdening others with one's own experiences, or failing to show reserve: "And it is for want of this reserve, that the one half of mankind make bad company to the other" (TMS 34.6).

Oh, and he comments on admiration of the rich and powerful: "This disposition to admire, and almost to worship, the rich and the powerful, and to despise, or, at least, to neglect persons of poor and mean condition...is...the great and most universal cause of the corruption of our moral sentiments" (TMS* 61.1).

On this head, Smith adds: "[N]ever come within the circle of ambition; nor ever bring yourself into comparison with those masters of the earth who have already engrossed the attention of half mankind before you" (TMS 57.7).

Now it seems as though Smith has passed 200 percent in his account of the sources of vice and disorders. But there's more— Smith writes of the ambitious pursuit of "place": "And thus, place... is the end of half the labours of human life; and is the cause of all the tumult and bustle, all the rapine and injustice, which avarice and ambition have introduced into this world" (TMS 57.8).

Finally, two more: "To be pleased with...groundless applause... is properly called vanity, and is the foundation of the most ridiculous and contemptible vices, the vices of affectation and common lying" (TMS 115.4)

And: "The propriety of our moral sentiments is never so apt to be corrupted, as when the indulgent and partial spectator is at hand, while the indifferent and impartial one is at a great distance" (TMS* 154.41).

Let's review: He points to at least nine sources of corruption and disorder: self-deceit, faction and fanaticism, false notions of religion, overrating the difference between one permanent situation and another, want of reserve, disposition to admire the rich and powerful, the pursuit of place or status, pleasure in groundless applause, and the impartial spectator being at a great distance.

It would seem that Smith is double- or triple-counting. Some of the overage can be chalked up to exaggeration. But there are two other ways to see the matter.

First, to explain corruption, Smith might be giving not only explanations, but also explanations of his explanations:

FIG. 19.1: LAYERED CORRUPTERS

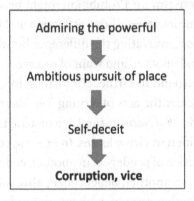

Admiring the powerful

Ambitious pursuit of place

Self-deceit

Corruption, vice

Admiring the powerful leads to the ambitious pursuit of place, which leads to self-deceit, which leads to corruption. Smith treats corruption with layers of explanation.

Indeed, when Smith writes of overrating the difference between one permanent situation and another, he immediately specifies three different manifestations of it: "Avarice over-rates the difference between poverty and riches: ambition, that between a private and a public station: vainglory, that between obscurity and extensive reputation" (TMS 149.31). Thus, the overrating of the difference between one permanent situation and another might manifest itself as the ambitious pursuit of place, or one of the other sources Smith has listed.

A second way to make sense of the matter is to see each source of corruption as a lens. When Smith says that self-deceit "is the source of half the disorders of human life," we might read that as: Half of the disorders of human life can be fruitfully interpreted through the self-deceit lens. That doesn't mean that such disorder cannot also be fruitfully interpreted through the faction and fanaticism lens, or the want-of-reserve lens, or any of the other lenses he exposits.

For example, take some Joe of 1919 who actively promoted Prohibition. Joe's activism for Prohibition might be viewed through several of the nine lenses—self-deceit, faction and fanaticism, false notions of religion, overrating the difference between one permanent situation and another, and want of reserve.

Now turn it around to virtue. For virtues, too, we have layers and lenses. Consider the acts of writing *The Theory of Moral Sentiments* and *The Wealth of Nations*—surely virtuous acts. But think how we may apply different virtue lenses. In one respect, the acts were the author's practice of prudence; in another, courage; in another, industriousness; in another, beneficence; also, more specifically, generosity; in another respect, perhaps gratitude—Adam Smith's gratitude to the creators of civilization.

CHAPTER 20

Adam Smith on Self-deceit

The University of Virginia Center for Politics, led by Larry Sabato, provides polling results that show deep social, political, and psychological divides between Biden voters and Trump voters (Kondik, Coleman, and Sabato 2021). Nowadays, it is common to think that large swaths of other people must be in denial.

"Oh yeah? — Well, I have a theory about *you!*"

In the old days, we argued over policy. Now we theorize about one another.

Adam Smith had things to say about denial and self-deceit. Here I draw exclusively from *The Theory of Moral Sentiments*. Applications are in your hands—and breast.

Employment implies an employer and an employee. We sometimes speak of someone being "self-employed," when employer and employee are the same person. Likewise, we sometimes speak of someone being "self-appointed," when appointer and appointee are the same person.

And we speak of "self-deceit," as though deceiver and deceivee are the same person. But that notion is paradoxical. If a fellow named Jim is both deceiver and deceivee, don't the deceiver and deceivee have the same knowledge? If so, how can the deceivee be deceived?

For the self-employed person, the employee knows that he is employed. And for the self-appointed person, the appointee knows that he is appointed. But for the self-deceived person, does the deceivee know that he is deceived?

The resolution comes by allowing a Jim1 separate from a Jim2, and allowing that Jim2 does not have the same knowledge as Jim1.

Jonathan Haidt (2012) speaks of subconscious activity as the elephant in the brain, and of consciousness as the rider, who fancies that he's steering the elephant. But the rider might do little more than rationalize where the elephant has taken him. My George Mason University economics colleague Robin Hanson and coauthor, Kevin Simler, have applied the idea pervasively in their book *The Elephant in the Brain: Hidden Motives in Everyday Life* (2017).

It is now well known that brain activity is divided and disjointed. As noted by Iain McGilchrist (2009, 187), scholars now say that consciousness accounts for no more than five percent of brain activity, and perhaps as little as one percent.

In discussing self-judgment, Smith writes: "I divide myself, as it were, into two persons…. The first is the judge; the second the person judged of" (TMS 113.6). Smith spoke of the conscience as "the man within the breast" and "the supposed impartial spectator." Sometimes our conscience nags us, as though one part of our being sees something that our conscious part has not faced up to.

Smith said we reflect on our own conduct and try to discern general rules of proper conduct. But Smith never said that there is a surefire method of discerning the rules of virtue. He never said the man within the breast knows virtue very well. He never said the man within the breast communicates effectively with our active, conscious self. He allowed that one part of Jim might deceive another part of Jim.

"When we are about to act," Smith wrote, "the eagerness of passion will seldom allow us to consider what we are doing with the candour of an indifferent person." Smith continues:

> The violent emotions which at that time agitate us, discolour our views of things, even when we are endeavouring to place ourselves in the situation of another, and to regard the objects that interest us in the light in which they will naturally appear to him. The fury of our own passions constantly calls us back to our own place, where every thing appears magnified and misrepresented by self-love. (TMS 157.3)

"When the action is over," he says, "and the passions which prompted it have subsided, we can enter more coolly into the sentiments of the indifferent spectator." But even after the action is over, we remain very sensitive about our prior conduct. By no means do we face up to our track record with candor:

> **The opinion which we entertain of our own character depends entirely on our judgment concerning our past conduct. It is so disagreeable to think ill of ourselves, that we often purposely turn away our view from those circumstances which might render that judgment unfavourable.** He is a bold surgeon, they say, whose hand does not tremble when he performs an operation upon his own person; and he is often equally bold who does not hesitate to pull off the mysterious

veil of self-delusion which covers from his view **the deformities of his own conduct.** Rather than see our own behaviour under so disagreeable an aspect, **we too often, foolishly and weakly, endeavour to exasperate anew those unjust passions which had formerly misled us**; we endeavour by artifice to awaken our old hatreds, and irritate afresh our almost forgotten resentments: we even exert ourselves for this miserable purpose, **and thus persevere in injustice,** merely **because we once were unjust,** and because **we are ashamed and afraid to see that we were so.** (TMS 157–158.4, emphasis added)

Denial itself becomes the new, present action of self-deceit. Our first self-deceit spawns a train of subsequent self-deceiving actions, which sustain the denial. Altogether we fall under "the mysterious veil of self-delusion."

Overcoming the veil of self-delusion is mighty difficult. Under the mysterious veil of self-delusion, we are stubborn. The deceiving elements of self may fend off even direct communication with a friend who knows better. Smith writes:

In order to pervert the rectitude of our own judgments concerning the propriety of our own conduct, it is not always necessary that the real and impartial spectator [that is, a flesh-and-blood friend who is impartial] should be at a great distance. When he is at hand, when he is present, the violence and injustice of our own selfish passions are sometimes sufficient to induce the man within the breast to make a report very different from what the real circumstances of the case are capable of authorizing. (TMS 156–157.1)

Those two sentences are the extent of Smith's play-by-play account of the event of self-deceit. A four-step diagram of that account is provided in Klein, Matson, and Doran (2018):

FIG. 20.1: SELF-DECEIT AT STAGES 3 AND 4, RESULTING IN A FAULTY REPORT FROM MWB (THE MAN WITHIN THE BREAST)

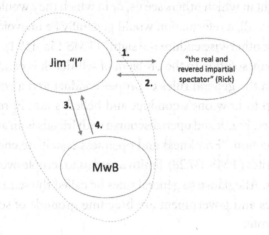

First, the conscious, walking, talking Jim tells his impartial friend Rick his rationalizations for his actions. Second, Rick responds and, with good counsel, perhaps disapproves of what Jim has done or is about to do. Third, Jim confers with his man within the breast. Fourth: "The violence and injustice of our own selfish passions are sometimes sufficient to induce the man within the breast to make a report very different from what the real circumstances of the case are capable of authorizing" (TMS 156–7).

Something has gone wrong, but it's not clear where. Maybe we should say that those selfish passions mislead the man within the breast. Maybe we should say that those selfish passions pressure or sway the man within the breast. The man within the breast returns "a report very different from what the real circumstances of the case are capable of authorizing." That the man within the breast can be misled or swayed in such fashion means that the man within the breast isn't as sound or sturdy as we might hope.

"This self-deceit, this fatal weakness of mankind," Smith writes, "is the source of half the disorders of human life. If we saw ourselves in the light in which others see us, or in which they would see us if they knew all, a reformation would generally be unavoidable. We could not otherwise endure the sight" (TMS 158–159.1).

The only solution to the problem of self-deceit is candid reflection upon the general rules of proper conduct and a courageous facing up to how one's conduct and beliefs stand in relation to those rules. Frank and open discourse with friends is an aid to such self-correction. "Frankness and openness conciliate confidence," Smith writes (TMS 337.28). Smith urged us to scruple over the general rules. Allegiance to general rules he called the sense of duty.

Politics and government are breeding grounds of self-deceit. Smith wrote:

> A true party-man hates and despises candour; and, in reality, there is no vice which could so effectually disqualify him for the trade of a party-man as that single virtue. The real, revered, and impartial spectator, therefore, is upon no occasion at a greater distance than amidst the violence and rage of contending parties…. Of all the corrupters of moral sentiments, therefore, faction and fanaticism have always been by far the greatest. (TMS 155–156.43)

It's no wonder that Smith put little faith in government as an agent of beneficial intervention. His political philosophy was rather different. The chief concern, he wrote, should be guarding against trouble: "The fatal effects of bad government arise from nothing, but that it does not sufficiently guard against the mischiefs which human wickedness gives occasion to" (TMS 187.1).

The main merit of Smith's political philosophy, wrote Friedrich Hayek, "is that it is a system under which bad men can do least harm" (1948, 11). Bad men sustain delusions to deny their self-deceptions. Smithian liberalism limits the evils that delusional men can wreak, and it tends to contest and correct their delusions in the first instance. That's why the delusional muzzle and repress their critics and usurp institutions: Their delusions would be unsustainable on impartial platforms and in open dialogue. Smithian liberalism is a prophylaxis against the evils of self-deceit.

CHAPTER 21

The Rule of Law

A blog post by my dear George Mason University colleague and friend Bryan Caplan begins:

> I've long been puzzled by libertarian reverence for "the rule of law." Why should friends of freedom care about the laws passed by the foolish and evil people who habitually rule over us? We should instead stubbornly put justice before the law.

I am a colleague and friend to Bryan and refer to him by his first name.

Bryan shows reverence for "justice" and "freedom" but not "the rule of law." He also shows no reverence for "law," which Bryan seems to flatten down to government law. Would Bryan regard that sacred justice or freedom to which he has dedicated much of his life as a sort of law?

Bryan expresses his own personal attitude toward government laws:

> What's the alternative [to dutifully following such laws]? Being a righteous scofflaw. Follow just laws. Break unjust laws when the expected gains are positive.

I agree with some of Bryan's points. Most importantly, Bryan encourages an exercise of conscience and discretion in the face of unjust laws. Unjust laws should not necessarily be followed. Don't be a heel-clicker.

But Bryan's opening remark—"I've long been puzzled by libertarian reverence for 'the rule of law'"—is jarring in its irreverence. A big problem with Bryan's post is that it makes law-following by citizens the central feature of the rule of law. Many of the commenters at the post rightly object. Many indicate what is more central to the concept of the rule of law.

The rule of law is something to honor, cherish, and elevate.

What is the rule of law? I don't attempt a definition but offer some hints.

The concept of the rule of law presupposes something like a polity with more than a semblance of jural integration and functionality. The supposition of jural integration means that we can speak of "the government" of "the polity," even if that polity, like the United States, involves an array of governments, like federal, state, and local. The presupposition of jural integration fits the concept of the modern nation-state. I note the presupposition because we don't want to apply the rule-of-law concept where it does not belong.

The rule-of-law concept involves the following three objects:

1.   the body of the laws that the government officializes—and posts on its website, as it were;

2.   the government's effectuating of—or administering of—that body of law, which involves:

     i. the posting of it on the website,

     ii. the enforcement of each law's precept,

     iii. the procedures, application, and execution of the sanctions;

3.   the conduct and attitudes of the subjects of the law.

Bryan's focus is law-following by citizens. That is part of the third object, the conduct of citizens. But the most central object of the rule-of-law concept is the effectuation.

Why do we expound on and extol the rule of law? Factions abuse the effectuation of law. They work things to gain and maintain power. They weaponize. They also abuse to enrich themselves, and to basely elevate themselves. A primary concern of the rule of law is the prevention of weaponization, bullying, double-standards, show trials, corruption, lying, cheating, election stealing, leaking information, stonewalling, deceit, conspiring, juntaism, and so on. The rule of law is about combatting abuse of powers that attend the making and effectuation of the law.

Factions are not equally vicious. Abusiveness tends to match the type of laws favored: Illiberality and anti-liberalism go together (Klein and Pino 2022), while liberality and liberalism go together (Matson 2022b). Virtuous politics is wise deliberation concerning the perennial political dilemma: the existence of public authority and the mitigation of its tremendous evils. "The fatal effects of bad government arise from nothing, but that it does not sufficiently guard against the mischiefs which human wickedness gives occasion to" (TMS 187.1).

Above, in speaking of effectuation, I used an old jurisprudential distinction between a law's precept and its sanction (a distinction found in Pufendorf, Carmichael, and Hutcheson). A law says, "*Don't–Or Else!*" The precept is the "Don't" and the sanction is the "or Else." Note that after a breach of the precept, the sanction involves a precept *for the sanctioner*, and that precept in turn suggests the sanctioning of the first-order sanctioner if he fails in his duty to apply the first-order sanction. Thus, the distinction recurs, generating a spiral.

If you think the deeper loops of this spiral are well defined, think again. It's a scary thought, in our world of weaponizers. That's one reason why the concept of the rule of law is important.

Again, effectuation of law is the most central object of the rule-of-law concept. Next would be the first object listed above, the body of law itself. Thus, what Bryan focuses on is part of the object that comes last in centrality, the conduct of the subjects of the law.

The rule-of-law concept is about the doings of government players, and only secondarily about whether citizens or subjects follow the law. Depravities in the body of law tend to breed both depredations in effectuation and law-breaking by subjects. So, although law-following is not primary in the rule-of-law concept, it relates to the things that are primary.

I like the old notion that a law is a rule laid down by a superior. What is a superior? One sort of superior is a jural superior, that is, the government in its lawmaking capacity (as opposed to its ownership capacity, i.e., public-sector resources and public administration). The government is a very special player. What other agent institutionalizes its coercions, posts them on a website, carries them out openly, and publicly pretends that the coercions are good for the whole? The term "superior" for this kind of player has a long tradition (Diesel 2020) and is worth embracing. We thusly regard the rules posted at the government website as law. The term *legal* signifies government rules with the status of law.

The government is not the only sort of superior, however. Theists call God's rules "laws." And nontheists, such as myself (an agnostic), may, in parallel fashion, call rules that are approved of by a worthy allegorical being, superior to any human being, "law":

> [T]hey are rules to direct the free actions of men: they are prescribed most surely by a lawful superior, and are

attended too with the sanction of rewards and punish-
ments. Those vicegerents of God within us never fail to
punish the violation of them by the torments of inward
shame and self-condemnation; and, on the contrary,
always reward obedience with tranquillity of mind, with
contentment, and self-satisfaction. (TMS 166.6)

If you go against the precept of one of the superior's laws, the
superior and his vicegerents disapprove of your conduct, and, for the
inspirited person, that disapproval functions as a sort of sanction.
The spirit's rules are reasonably fashioned "natural law" (see ch. 12).
The justice that wins Bryan's allegiance, too, may be thusly regarded as law on the same grounds—again, rule laid down by a superior.

Generally speaking, in a country like the United States, for the
ordinary citizen a government law ought to bring with it a certain
authority. The mere fact of legality ought to lead one, when consulting the scales, to add something in obligation, beyond common
prudence, to following the law. Adam Smith would agree with that
(e.g., TMS 81.8). Bryan's post seems to disagree. Compare with
Edmund Burke:

The people are not to be taught to think lightly of their
engagements to their governors; else they teach governors to think lightly of their engagements towards them.
In that kind of game in the end the people are sure to be
losers. (Burke 1992)

Existence without the rule of law is dystopic. The rule of law
gives warrant to liberalism. We should better learn to expound
on how liberalism promotes the rule of law and how the governmentalization of social affairs tends to destroy the rule of law. We

should better learn to expound on how governmentalization sucks.

"The rule of law" is a venerable expression for a worthy, if fuzzy, concept. Let us venerate the tradition that made Bryan possible:

6. "You shall not murder.

7. "You shall not commit adultery.

8. "You shall not steal.

9. "You shall not bear false witness against your neighbor.

10. "You shall not covet your neighbor's house; you shall not covet your neighbor's wife, nor his male servant, nor his female servant, nor his ox, nor his donkey, nor anything that is your neighbor's." (New King James Version of the Bible)

CHAPTER 22

Adam Smith's Essay on Language

I n reading Smith, it is helpful to think of a hermeneutic spiral:
our understanding of a part of a book informs our understanding of the whole, while, also, that of the whole informs that
of each part. Adding a part is not merely additive; it affects our
understanding of the new whole between the covers. Sometimes
the last chapter writes the first.

Smith's Language essay is a work "on which the author himself
set a high value," according to Dugald Stewart (EPS 292). It first
appeared in 1761 in *The Philological Miscellany*, Vol. I.[1] The full title
is: "Considerations concerning the first formation of Languages,
and the different genius of original and compounded Languages."
It was appended to TMS in 1767, the third edition, and noted on
the title page and in the table of contents, and remained part of
TMS—a vital part—so, it's a shame it was separated in the modern
Glasgow edition of Smith's works (it was moved to be with LRBL).

In his introduction to "Considerations," J. C. Bryce (1983, 25–26)
counts three considerations. First, there is the "conjectural" or
"theoretical" history of the development of a language, wherein sounds are used to signify concretes, and only gradually do
abstract sets of objects acquire signifiers. In an "original" language
(as opposed to a "compounded" one), inflections, typically agreeable to the ear, evolve to preserve unity of the event. Inflections are
word modifications such as declensions of nouns and adjectives and

1. The editor is not identified but probably was William Rose, who wrote a warm notice of
TMS in 1759 (Ross 2010, 198). In the Advertisement the editor wrote that "if he is encouraged to proceed" further volumes will appear, but none did.

conjugations of verbs. Inflections may express grammatical case, number, gender, tense, aspect, voice, and mood. In the advanced stages of an "original" language the inflections become complex.

Eighteenth-century English had resulted from twenty centuries of language groups crashing into one another, as Britain experienced wave after wave of invaders. The second consideration, Bryce explains, is what happens when different language groups crash into one another, and adults speaking different languages, now living together as a result of conquests and migrations, have to communicate with one another. The adult already thinks in terms of his native language, and it is terribly difficult for him to learn and remember all those darned inflections of languages new to him. In the attempt to communicate, inflections often get lopped off, and a compounded language emerges. The work that had been done by fine inflections now is done by separate words, notably prepositions and auxiliary verbs (for example, *can, could, may, might, must, shall, should, will, would, dare, need,* and *ought*). The several words must be in a certain order, whereas the fine inflections had allowed for "versification."[2] The more inflected languages left word order freer and made expression more concise and poetic.[3] Word order became constrained. Smith speaks of the compounding through time as the "composition" of the resultant language, and states his maxim about "the different genius of original and compounded Languages":

> In general it may be laid down for a maxim, that the more simple any language is in its composition, the more

2. Incidentally, we speculate that perhaps a language's inflections are a function also of the narrowness of writing, literacy, and printing in a society.

3. Smith's point about conciseness is borne out by flipping through Hutcheson (2007), with the Latin on verso and the English on recto: The Latin side consistently has empty space at the bottom of the page.

complex it must be in its declensions and conjugations; and, on the contrary, the more simple it is in its declensions and conjugations, the more complex it must be in its composition. (LRBL 221–222).

The third consideration explained by Bryce is an overall assessment of, say, Latin[4] versus English. Things have been gained, as adult newcomers to English more easily join in. But things have been lost. The final words of the essay say that Latin's conciseness, versification, and sweetness made perfection of beauty much more acquirable "than it can be to those whose expression is constantly confined by the prolixness, constraint, and monotony of modern languages" (LRBL 226). These final words strike a dour note. Since the essay is an appendix which concludes TMS, that work itself ends on that dour note.

This final phrase—"confined by the prolixness, constraint, and monotony of modern languages"—brings to mind the final words of WN, that Great Britain should "endeavour to accommodate her future views and designs to the real mediocrity of her circumstances" (WN, 947.92). The prophet of the modern, commercial, liberal society does not conclude with a zeal for progress. There is no promise of an integral, poetic life. In the Language essay, Smith explains, "mankind have learned by degrees to **split and divide** almost every event into a great number of metaphysical parts, expressed by the different parts of speech, variously combined in the different members of every phrase and sentence" (LRBL 217, emphasis added). Dividing and subdividing is a main theme in WN. It is a central point of the Language essay, and we may read it into

4. Latin is referred to abundantly in Smith's essay. While highly inflected, it is by no means regarded by him as the most purely "original" language. He writes: "The Latin is a composition of the Greek and of the ancient Tuscan languages. Its declensions and conjugations accordingly are much less complex than those of the Greek" (LRBL 222).

the rest of TMS. TMS and WN both end on a dour note.

Smith explained that in Latin the inflections afforded expression of an event "as it appears in nature, not as something **separated and detached**" (LRBL 211, emphasis added). In the modern compounded language, separate words—prepositions, helping verbs, adverbs, exclamations, etc.—represent specific ideas, images, relations, and sentiments. An aspect of an object is turned into another separate object, and tagged. Each word is then combined with others, the collection ordered to fit the event. That contrast is then projected to life, as Smith moves from the more communal focus of TMS to the great society of WN. In modern life, the stream of experience is not the flowing of integral wholes, but a sequence of events, objects, and relations "separated and detached." Elements are subdivided, distinguished, and tagged. Social and jural relations become individuated. Our agreements have self-generated terms and conditions, and our estates consist of myriad personal effects. Each person stewards his own assemblage. There are still natural families and neighbors, but we often have not seen our siblings in many months and do not know the neighbor. That's modernity, and we must make the most of it. That's the note on which Smith concludes both his two great works.

TMS takes up man as known to recorded history. Although there is discussion of "barbarians" and "savages" of recorded history, and although the idea of natural selection plays a theoretical role in cultural evolution (TMS 211.16, 77.10, 87.6, 142.13), there is almost nothing reaching back earlier, along the lines of the four-stage theory of social development. The book does not raise conjectures about early man's existence in hunter bands. But the Language essay does—its story starts prior to language. It speaks of nouns and verbs being "coëval" (LRBL, 215), since a noun and a verb are both necessary in either affirming or denying something's existence. Smith continued with deeper-evolution ideas in WN, the lectures on jurisprudence (check "hunters" in the index), and to some extent in LRBL when he discusses the communal and musical origins of poetry (LRBL 136–139).

The appending of the Language essay to TMS helps to make explicit deeper-evolution ideas that had been only implicit in TMS. In the Language essay, Smith writes: "The general rule would establish itself insensibly, and by slow degrees" (211). Such development parallels the spontaneous generation of proprieties in TMS. Indeed, language norms live in discourse, and discourse is a form of conduct, so language norms *are* proprieties. In discoursing, one's semantics and syntax can be praiseworthy or blameworthy, virtuous or vicious. And the point extends further. As Marcelo Dascal (2006, 101) puts it: "[Smith's] rhetoric is a theory of the propriety of *linguistic* action." The Language essay shows how the propriety of linguistic action depends on history, and in that way the essay underscores TMS's teaching that history plays a role inside of moral theory.

The Language essay may be said to have introduced conjectural history into Smith's published works, although TMS's remarks about the formation of religious beliefs "[d]uring the ignorance and darkness of pagan superstition" (164.4) might qualify as a bit of conjectural history. Chris Berry (1974, 133) places Smith in the "Organic" school of the origin of language, in contrast most notably to the "Theological" and "Rationalist" schools.

Also, the Language essay treats grammar, which plays a critical role in TMS. There is but one virtue whose rules are grammar-like, and that virtue is commutative justice. Its precepts against messing with other people's stuff are "precise and accurate." The rules of other virtues are "loose, vague, and indeterminate" (TMS 327.1, 175.11). A shared grammar is crucial for communication, and a shared social grammar is crucial for peace and the pursuit of happiness in modern life. "Smith's message is crystal clear: moral philosophy requires the two different types of rule" (Dascal 2006, 103). The Language essay underscores the specialness of commutative justice. And it quietly suggests that a system of commutative justice is, like a grammar, a set of emergent conventions.

CHAPTER 23

The Music of Social Intercourse: Synchrony in Adam Smith

By Daniel Klein and Michael J. Clark

I n an article in *Psychological Science* entitled "Synchrony and Cooperation," Scott C. Wiltermuth and Chip Heath (2009) tell how marching, singing, and dancing conduce to cooperation. They report on three experiments showing that greater cooperation in public-goods games came in the variant in which subjects either had previously been put to marching together (as opposed to walking normally) or were singing or moving in synchrony. They note that "[t]he idea that synchronous movement improves group cohesion has old roots" (1) and cite Emile Durkheim and several more recent works of historical anthropology and psychology.

Here we examine the place of language denoting musicality or synchrony in the works of Adam Smith. His first book, *The Theory of Moral Sentiments*, is suffused with the sense that synchrony is fundamental to human sympathy, cooperation, and well-being. We explore the place of synchrony or harmony in Smith's writings and visions, and discuss the relationship between *The Theory of Moral Sentiments* and *The Wealth of Nations*.

Sympathy as shared sentiment

Adam Smith's moral theory considers a number of sources of moral approval and at each turn he posits or invokes an accompanying spectator. In judging an action, at each turn we consult our sympathy with a spectator that is proper or natural to the occasion. Smith's idea of sympathy is "fellow-feeling" (TMS 10.5). The sentiment is shared, it exists as a common experience, much like the beat of a chant or melody of a song, neither mine, nor yours, but ours. To convey this notion of coordination Smith often used synchronous figures of speech, as when our sentiments "keep time together."

The terms used include *keeping* or *beating time*, *concord* and *discord*, *pitch*, and, most importantly, *harmony*. Table 1 shows the number of occurrences of musical or synchronous terms in reference to sentiment coordination.

TABLE 23.1: OCCURRENCES IN TMS OF MUSICAL OR SYNCHRONOUS TERMS IN DISCUSSING COORDINATED SENTIMENT

Term	Occurrences
Accord	2
Beat(s) Time	4
Concord	14
Dances	1
Discord, Discordant	8
Dissonance	2
Harmony, Harmonious	21
Keep(s/ing) Time	7
Melody (ious)	1
Motion	5
Move, Movement	5
Music, Musical	4
Pitch	7
Sing	2
Song	4

Tone	2
Tune	1
Unisons	1
TOTAL	91

Synchronous language is found at important places in Smith's thought

Besides being pervasive in Smith's first book, synchronous language pertains especially to things most significant in his thought. Smith simply posits the human yearning for sympathy, the importance of which can hardly be overstated. Smith speaks of a "character...so detestable as that of one who takes pleasure to sow dissension among friends." Smith asks: "Yet wherein does the atrocity of this so much abhorred injury consist?"

> It is in depriving them of that friendship itself, in robbing them of each other's affections, from which both derived so much satisfaction; it is in disturbing **the harmony** of their hearts, and putting an end to that happy commerce which had before subsisted between them. These affections, that **harmony**, this commerce, are felt...to be of more importance to happiness than all the little services which could be expected to flow from them. (TMS 39.1)

We highlight synchronous terms by putting them in bold. Smith elaborates an example of a man who has suffered an offense:

> He longs for that relief which nothing can afford him but the entire **concord** of the affections of the spectators with his own. To see the emotions of their hearts, in every respect, **beat time** to his own, in the violent and

disagreeable passions, constitutes his sole consolation.
(TMS 22.7)

Smith explains that our yearning for sympathy leads us to modulate our own sentiments and passions. Continuing from the preceding quotation, he states:

> But he can only hope to obtain this by lowering his passion to that **pitch** in which the spectators are capable of going along with him. He must flatten, if I may be allowed to say so, the sharpness of its natural **tone**, in order to reduce it to **harmony** and **concord** with the emotions of those who are about him. (TMS 22.7)

Early in TMS, Smith distinguishes two sets of virtues. The virtues of modulating our passions belong to "the great, the awful and respectable" virtues "of self-denial, of self-government." The other side of the human spiral consists of "[t]he soft, the gentle, the amiable virtues," from which we indulge the sentiments and passions of others:

> And hence it is, that to feel much for others and little for ourselves, that to restrain our selfish, and to indulge our benevolent affections, constitutes the perfection of human nature; and can alone produce among mankind that **harmony** of sentiments and passions in which consists their whole grace and propriety. (TMS 25.5)

The title of the book's third chapter indicates the prominent place that synchronous figures have in Smith's thinking: "*Of the manner in which we judge of the propriety or impropriety of the affections of other men, by their* **concord** *or* **dissonance** *with our own*" (TMS 16).

Such concord is not mere grease on the wheels of society, but part of the stuff of human fulfillment:

> The great pleasure of conversation and society, besides, arises from a certain correspondence of sentiments and opinions, from a certain **harmony** of minds, which like so many **musical** instruments coincide and **keep time** with one another. But this most delightful **harmony** cannot be obtained unless there is a free communication of sentiments and opinions. (TMS 337.28)

Synchronous figures, finally, are used in Smith's vision of a complex commercial society. The latter is developed in *The Wealth of Nations* but also plays a crucial part in *TMS*. In a famous passage, Smith faults "the man of system" "who seems to imagine that he can arrange the different members of a great society with as much ease as the hand arranges the different pieces upon a chess-board":

> He does not consider that the pieces upon the chess-board have no other principle of motion besides that which the hand impresses upon them; but that, in the great chess-board of human society, every single piece has a principle of motion of its own, altogether different from that which the legislature might chuse to impress upon it. If those two principles coincide and act in the same direction, the game of human society will go on easily and **harmoniously**, and is very likely to be happy and successful. If they are opposite or different, the game will go on miserably, and the society must be at all times in the highest degree of disorder. (TMS 234.17)

WN under TMS's umbrella

The vision of complex commercial society as a harmonious system runs us into old issues about the relationship between TMS and WN. It has long been said there are significant tensions between the two works. Certain nineteenth-century German scholars highlighted or even exaggerated some of the differences, creating what became known as "*das Adam Smith problem*" (see the editor's introduction to TMS by D. D. Raphael and Alec L. Macfie, 20ff). There are major differences in the tone and feeling, and, as Peter Minowitz (1993; 2004) highlights, the talk of providence that pervades TMS all but disappears in *WN*.

The difference in tone and feeling is confirmed by examining whether TMS's synchronous terms occur in WN. Remarkably, they, too, all but disappear. Of the 18 TMS synchronous terms reported in Table 1, the occurrence of like usage in WN for 16 of them *is a big fat zero*, while "concord" has one occurrence and "discord" two. One of those passages emanates the warmth of TMS:

> By such [mercantilist/protectionist] maxims as these, however, nations have been taught that their interest consisted in beggaring all their neighbours. Each nation has been made to look with an invidious eye upon the prosperity of all the nations with which it trades, and to consider their gain as its own loss. Commerce, which ought naturally to be, among nations, as among individuals, a bond of union and friendship, has become the most fertile source of **discord** and animosity. (WN 493.9)

But such moments of warmth are rare in WN.[1] The differ-

---

1. E.g., "the good cheer of private families" (WN, 440).

ence between the feeling of TMS and that of WN is perhaps best summed up by the fact that in WN, the word *sentiment(s)* occurs just twice—in the famous passage on the enfeebling effects of routine specialized labor (WN 782.50), and in a passage on teacher motivation (WN 760.6)—and *sympathy/sympathetic* occurs not at all.

Vivienne Brown (1994, 46) has observed that one of the most central ideas in TMS, the *impartial spectator*—the idealized universal spectator, whose characterization is incomplete, uncertain, and disputed yet is represented in some way as our conscience—makes no appearance in WN. Does the impartial spectator's presence in TMS but absence from WN speak of a conflict between the two works?

We are inclined to say—as most Smith scholars today do—that there is no fundamental conflict between TMS and WN. Despite its cooler feeling and handling of social affairs, WN is, in our view, part of TMS's broader ethical plexus. WN comes within TMS's umbrella.

In a key passage in TMS, Smith summarizes the ethical plexus of his work as involving "four sources" of moral approval. We highlight here only the fourth and broadest source:

> ...we approve of any character or action..., last of all, when we consider such actions as making a part of a system of behaviour which tends to promote the happiness either of the individual or of the society, they appear to derive a beauty from this utility, not unlike that which we ascribe to any well-contrived machine. (TMS 326.16)

With reference to promotion of the happiness of the society, Smith here throws ethics open to consequences wide and abstract. Most of the morality plays in TMS are of a private nature, interaction among neighbors or "equals,"[2] where the wide social view plays little role. That is why the impartial spectator is usually thought to be a personal moral advisor, not a political economist. WN, however, was an annex to TMS, making together a more extensive system of moral sentiments. WN explores the broad view in TMS's fourth source especially as concerns commercial behavior and public policy.

In explicating the fourth source, Smith did not use synchronous language. But elsewhere he invokes similar imagery and does: "Human society, when we contemplate it in a certain abstract and philosophical light, appears like a great, an immense machine, whose regular and **harmonious movements** produce a thousand agreeable effects" (TMS 316.2).

In TMS, Smith enlarges on how "regard to the beauty of order, of art and contrivance, frequently serves to recommend those institutions which tend to promote the public welfare" (TMS 185.11). Only by pondering and studying the workings of society do we learn to see, in an abstract way, the larger unintended consequences of individual action. "Nothing tends so much to promote public spirit as the study of politics, of the several systems of civil government, their advantages and disadvantages, of the constitution of our own country, its situation…its commerce." (TMS 186.11). Thus, "political disquisitions, if just, and reasonable, and practicable, are of all the works of speculation the most useful" (TMS 187.11).

In that sense, contrary to what Vivienne Brown observes, perhaps the impartial spectator *does* appear in *The Wealth of Nations—as the author*. For, if the inmate within the reader's breast is its rep-

2. As noted by the TMS editors D. D. Raphael and A. L. Macfie (p. 40), from the fourth edition (1774) on, the title page included a description of the work: "The Theory of Moral Sentiments, Or An Essay towards an Analysis of the Principles by which Men naturally judge concerning the Conduct and Character, **first of their Neighbours,** and afterwards of themselves" (emphasis added).

resentative, and if "To direct the judgments of this inmate is the great purpose of all systems of morality" (TMS 293.47; see also 329.6), then the author of such a system, if edifying and properly so, would be akin to the impartial spectator. *The Wealth of Nations*, then, strives for greater harmony among us as we contemplate political systems, public policy, and commercial activity. In WN, Smith never speaks of sympathy. It is for the reader, in his encounter with Smith's mind, to discover sympathy, or not.

Concords: "all that is wanted or required"

We should be mindful that, as noted by Frederick Maitland (1875, 132), Smith was well aware of society's inherent disharmonies. Smith says: "What are the common wages of labour depends every where upon the contract usually made between [workmen and masters], whose interests are by no means the same. The workmen desire to get as much, the masters to give as little as possible" (WN 83). Disharmonies arise also in rivalrous competition and man's impulse toward creativity and improvement. Yet Smith sees a preserve of sentimental concord "sufficient for the **harmony** of society." "Though they will never be **unisons,** they may be **concords** and this is all that is wanted or required" (TMS 22.7).

Charles Griswold (1999), who explores the musical metaphors in *The Theory of Moral Sentiments*,[3] argues that Smith sought a larger enlightened frame within which we could sufficiently harmonize our toleration and testing of lower-frame disharmonies, a larger frame that emphasized commutative justice and natural liberty. To represent Smith's aesthetic aspiration of higher harmony by means of enlightenment, Griswold (1999, 75, 332) aptly quotes from Smith's essay on the imitative arts (which discusses music at length):

3. In Griswold (1999), see 74-5, 111-2, 120-7, 183, 196-7, 211-3, 327-48, 373-5.

In the contemplation of that immense variety of agreeable and melodious sounds, arranged and digested, both
in their coincidence and in their succession, into so complete and regular a system, the mind in reality enjoys not
only a very great sensual, but a very high intellectual,
pleasure, not unlike that which it derives from the contemplation of a great system in any other science. (EPS
204-5)

Griswold nicely captures the dialectic element in Smith's vision
of social harmony: We consider "actions as being parts of a larger unity and system because of the imagination's restless drive for
order" (1999, 339).

Evolutionary origins?

Smith said we feel benevolence toward some people more than
toward others—Sandra Peart and David Levy (2005) aptly refer to
the "sympathetic gradient" in Smith's moral ecology. First comes
oneself. Next come one's family members, who when living in the
same house "are more habituated to sympathize" with one another.
After the self and the family, Smith proceeds to friendships, neigh-
borhoods, "orders and societies" within civil society, the nation,
and finally "universal benevolence" or humanity (TMS 219–37).
Our concern for others is based on social bonds or social distance,
measured in terms of shared experiences and likenesses.

Smith (TMS 237.6, 77.10) suggests that nature has thusly directed our concern to where it can be most helpful, for with social
nearness comes *better knowledge and understanding* of how to make
benevolence effective. In the experiments conducted by Wiltermuth and Heath (2009) the synchronies *did not* enhance any knowl-

edge about how to increase joint payoffs in subsequent play. But Smith is describing our instincts or psychological tendencies, and the mere fact of having been "more habituated to sympathize" with one another, strengthening social bonds would naturally prompt greater cooperation.

Wiltermuth and Heath say that "existing hypotheses about why synchrony works seem limited" (1). Smith's point about local knowledge might figure into an evolutionary explanation. If the early human being depended on group selection (Hayek 1988; Sober and Wilson 1998; Zywicki 2000; Field 2004), one who cooperated with those who were socially near would tend to prosper, particularly if expulsion, stoning, withholding of food, or other forms of punishment were visited upon the non-cooperator. The beings that survived are those for whom synchronous behavior habituates sympathy, increases social nearness, and conduces to greater cooperation.

Other metaphors in TMS

Although synchrony pervades TMS, the primary idea is coordinated sentiment. That idea is developed by several kinds of metaphor. Foremost is an imagined face-to-face expression of agreement or sympathy, between the one who is to render judgment and the supposed companion who also sees the actions judged of. That is, in judging the actions of Timothy, you consult, as it were, an imagined spectator, and it is a sense of face-to-face agreement with this accompanying spectator that is most distinctive to Smith. Also pervasive in TMS are the metaphors of "entering into" or "going along with" another's sentiments. While synchrony suggests hearing and timing, spectatorship suggests seeing and vision, and "enter into" and "go along with" suggest little narratives of making company. Thus, Smith invokes many modes of common experience in developing the idea of coordinated sentiment. But synchrony is certainly central.

CHAPTER 24

Isn't It Odd? 21 Prompts to Reading Adam Smith between the Lines

U p to about 2010, little scholarship on Adam Smith delved into his esotericism. A writer writes esoterically when her text affords both an obvious meaning and, "between the lines," a nonobvious meaning. The nonobvious meaning need not be in conflict with the obvious meaning, but sometimes it is, in which case the obvious meaning should be discounted.

Eso- means interior (from Greek) and *exo-* means exterior. When the text has two meanings, the obvious meaning is called the exoteric meaning.

Here I compile 21 items that might represent esoteric moments in Smith's texts. Each item prompts thought of a nonobvious meaning, sometimes just a bit of humor or irony. Calling attention to the punchlines of a set of jokes is not particularly agreeable. But perhaps it is useful. Esoteric writing calls for esoteric reading.

But sometimes esoteric readers see esotericism where they should not. Sometimes the obvious meaning is all there is. Sometimes an oddity or irregularity in the text is not intended by the author. Sometimes "Homer nods," as the saying goes.

But surely most of the following 21 instances from the writings of Adam Smith involve multiple meanings or irony. Readers need to be prepared to read Smith esoterically. Most of the entries that follow offer a citation that speak to the esotericism of the passage.

Items pertaining to Smith's early essays:

1. Isn't it odd that Smith should conclude a long essay (EPS 105) on how surprise, wonder, and admiration prompt scientific inquiry by expressing his own surprise at how he himself has "been insensibly drawn in" to speaking and talking in a manner directly contrary to that in which he had set out to treat his subject, the history of astronomy? (See Matson 2018.) And isn't it odd how the question that ends the essay ends with a period, not a question mark?

2. Isn't it odd that in the second of a seeming series of twelve rhetorical questions—a series uncharacteristic in its rabidness—Smith would seemingly suggest that Aristotle, "that great philosopher," "appears to have been so much superior to his master [Plato] in every thing but eloquence," when Smith shows greater preoccupation with and affinity to Plato? Might the phrasing "that great philosopher" and "his master" (EPS 122-23n*) signify, not Aristotle and Plato, but Plato and Socrates? And isn't it odd that among the twelve apparent rhetorical questions, this one, *and this one only*, does not end with a question mark?[1]

3. Isn't it odd how Smith writes:

   I shall only add, that the dedication [of Rousseau's *Discourse on Inequality*] to the republic of

---

1. I think of the sentence in Hume's Conclusion to Book I of the *Treatise*, beginning "But does it follow...," which seems at first to be a question and likewise lacks a question mark (the editors of the 2007 Clarendon edition, D. F. Norton and M. F. Norton, changed Hume's punctuation to a question mark—wrongly, I feel).

> Geneva, of which Mr. Rousseau has the hon-
> our of being a citizen, is an agreeable, ani-
> mated, and I believe too, a just panegyric; and
> expresses that ardent and passionate esteem
> which becomes a good citizen to entertain for
> the government of his country and the char-
> acter of his countrymen. (EPS 254)

directly after quoting Rousseau saying that for
today's "man of society" everything is "reduced to
appearances, every thing becomes factitious and
acted," that "we have nothing but a deceitful and
frivolous exterior; honour without virtue, reason
without wisdom, and pleasure without happiness"?
(See Klein 2014.)

4. Isn't it amusing that, in illustrating how Samuel
   Johnson might have undertaken his *Dictionary* so as
   to better illustrate the polysemy and multiple uses
   of a word, Smith (EPS 241) should furnish model
   entries for the words *but* and *humour*, and say at the
   end of his review that "those who are under any
   difficulty" in determining the use of a word have
   recourse to Johnson's *Dictionary* "but by which the
   determination is rendered easy"?

The Wealth of Nations

5. Isn't it odd that, when Smith endorses the status-quo policy of a ceiling on interest rates, saying
   that without such ceiling "[s]ober people...would

not venture into the competition" for loans, he then immediately says that under the status-quo policy "sober people are universally preferred, as borrowers, to prodigals and projects"? If creditors can discern soberness with the ceiling, why wouldn't they be able to discern soberness without a ceiling? (WN 357.15; see Diesel 2021.)

6. Isn't it odd that Smith saw blooming dynamism in the Glasgow of the 1750s and yet in the *Wealth of Nations* tends to portray market forces as rather placid? Isn't it odd that he remarks repeatedly on how free markets enkindle discovery of the previously unthought-of, bringing new markets and downward shifts in costs, but never highlights the dynamism of market forces? (See DelliSanti 2021.)

7. Isn't it odd that in the midst of propounding (WN 65.23–3) that "the quantity of labour commonly employed in acquiring or producing any commodity, is the only circumstance which can regulate the quantity of labour which it ought commonly to purchase, command, or exchange for," Smith should explain that labour varies by its severity, dexterity, skill, ingenuity, and esteem, heterogeneities that not only mark the "advanced state of society" but that "must probably have taken place in its earliest and rudest period"? Isn't it odd, then, that Smith should theorize using some homogeneous-unit-of-labor concept when he says that labor has from the very start been heterogeneous? (See Robinson and Subrick 2021.)

8. Isn't it odd that Smith should write (WN 782.50)

of the degenerate state into which "the labouring poor" must descend "unless government takes some pains to prevent it" and seem to endorse some government financing of schooling, and yet in his final words (815.5) on the subject say that the expense for schooling "might perhaps with equal propriety, and even with some advantage, be defrayed altogether by those who receive the immediate benefit of such education and instruction, or by the voluntary contribution of those who think they have occasion for either the one or the other"? (See Drylie 2021; 2020.)

The Theory of Moral Sentiments

9. Isn't it odd that, in recounting a story about Antimachus discoursing before an audience including Plato, Smith should replace Antimachus with Parmenides, even though Smith knew that Parmenides could never have addressed Plato? (TMS 253.31; see Murphy and Humphries 2021.)

10. Isn't it odd that in TMS Part II, Section II, Smith should treat commutative justice as justice *simpliciter*, as though commutative justice is the only proper meaning of "justice" and yet go on to use "justice" pervasively also in two other senses, and in the final part of the book to affirm all three senses of "justice"? (See Klein 2021.)

11. Isn't it odd that Smith should mention reputation as something covered by commutative justice, but make no mention of reputation just two pages later when he elaborates the "most sacred laws" of com-

mutative justice? Isn't it odd that he would some-times include reputation, even though he knew that reputation did not fit the hallmark of commutative justice, namely that its laws are "precise and accurate"? (See Bonica and Klein 2021.)

12. Isn't it odd that Smith should say that we labor under a "deception" that wealth will make us happy, while he justifies self-approval for our having done deeds that augment our wealth? (TMS 183.10; see Matson 2021.)

13. Isn't it odd how Smith ends that same disquisition by referring to "the beggar, who suns himself by the side of the highway," without identifying the particular beggar alluded to? (TMS 185.10; see Martin 2014.)

14. Isn't it odd that Smith (TMS 330.9) should introduce "a trite example: a highwayman, by the fear of death, obliges a traveller to promise him a certain sum of money," devote fully two-and-a-half pages to "Whether such a promise, extorted in this manner by unjust force, ought to be regarded as obligatory," and then conclude the penultimate paragraph of the section (and of the book, apart from the appended essay on language): "Systems of positive law, therefore, though they deserve the greatest authority, as the records of the sentiments of mankind in different ages and nations, yet can never be regarded as accurate systems of the rules of natural justice"?

15. Isn't it odd that in expositing the error of introduc-

ing "frivolous accuracy" into "subjects which do not admit of it" (TMS 340.33), Smith (333.16) should make as his target the books of casuistry of "the Roman Catholic superstition"?

16. Isn't it odd that, in Part IV of TMS, in representing his friend's moral theory, Smith should obscure half of it, the agreeableness half, as opposed to the usefulness (or "utility") half, especially as Smith's enhancement, fittingness or propriety, is so frequently couched by Smith as a species of agreeableness? (See Matson, Doran, and Klein 2019.)

17. Isn't it odd that in illustrating, when it comes to "particular usages," that people can accept and even endorse a most "horrible practice" (TMS 209.12, 211.16), Smith should highlight a practice of ancient Greece, infanticide, a practice he even finds justification for in certain circumstances, while just a few pages earlier he rebuked an ongoing atrocity perpetrated by his fellow countrymen in his own time? (See chapter 7.)

18. Isn't it odd that the seemingly distinct sources of vice, corruption, and disorder mentioned in TMS should reach to nine and yet each be so eminent?

- one "the great and most universal cause" (TMS 61.1),

- another "the cause of...all the rapine and injustice" (TMS 57.8),

- another "the foundation of the most ridiculous and contemptible vices" (TMS 115.4),

- another almost the only cause "which can

occasion any very gross perversion of our natural sentiments" (TMS176.12),

- another "by far the greatest" of all corrupters (TMS 156.43),

- another "[t]he great source of both the misery and disorders of human life" (TMS 149.31),

- another "the source of half the disorders of human life" (TMS 158-159.1),

- another the source of half the ill company we make to one another (TMS 34.6),

- and yet another that makes it most apt that "[t]he propriety of our moral sentiments...be corrupted" (TMS 154.41).

And isn't it odd that four of these nine remarks were new to Ed 6 of 1790? (See chapter 19.)

19. Isn't it odd that Smith, in noting that we use "reason and philosophy" to defend ourselves "against fear and anxiety, the great tormentors of the human breast," should say, and at the very opening of his moral philosophy (TMS 12.12), that we do so "in vain"?

20. Given the connection in Hume between speculation and practice—"philosophical decisions are nothing but the reflections of common life, methodized and corrected" (Hume 2000)—"The end of all moral speculations is to...beget correspondent habits" (Hume 1998, 5)—and likewise Edmund Burke—"the End of all speculation should be prac-

tice of one sort or another" (Burke 1957, 82)—, and given Smith's own emphasis on the moral duty to estimate ideas properly, and on rooting principles in "particular instances," and on habitual practice as essential to virtue, and given his presentation of "men of speculation" as practicing a "business or a particular trade," isn't it odd that Smith should say (TMS 315.3) that the determination of a certain philosophical issue (namely, by what power or faculty in the mind is virtuous conduct recognized and recommended to us) is "of the greatest importance in speculation" but "none in practice"? (See Matson, Doran, and Klein 2019.)

21. Isn't it odd that at just about the dead-center of the first edition of the volumes containing WN and of the last edition of the volumes containing TMS there appears the same 6-gram, "led by an invisible hand to"? (See Klein and Lucas 2011.)

CHAPTER 25

Dangers of Mere-liberty

Chapter 17 explored meanings of liberty. The spine of the classical liberal meaning is government not messing with one's stuff. In treating David Hume, Erik Matson and I (2020) speak of "mere-liberty" for that idea. In this chapter, I offer a few words about why even exponents of classical liberalism often treat that idea only indirectly.

Nicholas Capaldi and Gordon Lloyd (2016) offer a cycle at the heart of what they call the liberty narrative: $TP \rightarrow ME \rightarrow LG \rightarrow RL \rightarrow CPA \rightarrow TP$.

TP stands for the technological project.

ME stands for the market economy.

LG stands for limited government (restraining government on behalf of individual liberty).

RL stands for rule of law.

CPA stands for the culture of personal autonomy.

(Capaldi and Lloyd 2016, 2)

They are basically right, and the package does indeed represent transformative developments, not just the Great Enrichment, but really new troubling and frightening human conditions. Due to some of the troubling conditions, "the Liberal Creed" was famously condemned by Karl Polanyi (1944), but the profound criticisms and doubts go back a long way.

The claim to be able to live without others messing with one's stuff is so strong in equal-equal jural relationships (you and your neighbor) that to even suggest a parallel in superior-inferior jural relationships, and to denominate that parallel in some fashion, such as *liberty*, is bound to suggest claims of parallel strength. Even when one takes pains to say otherwise, one is apt to be misunderstood and misrepresented. After all, although the commutative-justice delineations of "stuff," "one's," and "messing with" evolve toward precision and accuracy, as Hume taught us (and proving that they are "artificial"),[1] the limitations, the hedges, the judicious stays and cautions, remain but loose, vague, and indeterminate, and are often given less than justice. Simple principles may give rise to slogans, men of system, and men of faction. "[A] man has but a bad grace, who delivers a theory, however true, which he must confess leads to a practice dangerous and pernicious" (Hume 1998, 279).[2]

The liberty principle is, for many, frightening, and, for others, intoxicating. Intoxication exacerbates the trouble, and the fright. The liberty principle is an engine of policy formulation and criticism. It is an axe that can be swung at any established general rules contravening the principle. Bentham (1787) swung that axe on usury laws—with a rationalistic eschewal of writing between the lines. Perhaps Smith had looked to others to unfold, in due course, liberal discourse and liberal reform.

1. See the *Treatise* pp. 529–533, including the following passage highlighting the *specialness* of commutative justice's precise and accurate rules: "'Twas, therefore, with a view to this inconvenience, that men have establish'd those principles, and have agreed to restrain themselves by general rules, which are unchangeable by spite and favour, and by particular views of private or public interest. These rules, then, are artificially invented for a certain purpose, and are contrary to the common principles of human nature, which accommodate themselves to circumstances, and have no stated invariable method of operation."

2. For some moments in the *History* (1983) of Hume speaking to esotericism, see III, 232, 433; V, 544. See also the Hume passages in Melzer's online appendix http://press.uchicago.edu/sites/melzer/melzer_appendix.pdf.

The flavor is an acquired taste and the brew is a heady one, associated with frightening gateways. In many ways the flavor goes against our basic nature and instincts, something that I think Hume, Rousseau, and Smith recognized.

One need not think about radical assault, like that of the Lockean-anarchist author feigned by Burke in *A Vindication of Natural Society* (1756). The idea of just some serial abolitions would astonish 1750 readers: Abolition of slavery and slave-trade, equal liberty for women, the end of vocational corporations/guilds. Had not greater freedom in religion produced a most alarming pandemic of *Gangræna* (Edwards 1646)?

Today we find alarm over the notion of liberalizing gay marriage, prostitution, drugs, guns, human organs, 10-cent wage rates, and so on. Espousers of liberty open themselves to charges of defending the undefendable: merciless usurers, perverts, greedy merchants and capitalists, abettors of abortion and suicide. One is tarred with forsaking virtue for acquisitiveness, high things for low things. Hume in fact pulled his essay on suicide (in which he uses "native liberty" and "our natural liberty," 1987, 580, 588 n6), "faced with the prospect of ecclesiastical condemnation and perhaps even official prosecution."[3]

If a circa-1750 author wished to advance the centrality of mere-liberty, and wanted to make his voice appealing to a wide and future readership, and wanted to gain an appointment at Edinburgh or Glasgow, he might well have wished to obscure mere-liberty to some extent, and to understate his support for it. He may also have wished to downplay consequences that tend to flow from liberalization, such as innovation, mobility, dynamism, and other moral and cultural consequences like those decried by Polanyi. Just how much independence of judgment, how much autonomy, do

3. E.F. Miller's editorial note on p. 577 of the *Essays*.

individuals really want to be responsible for? It is no wonder that great taboos surround mere-liberty.

The Hume literature features many works (Winters 1979; Livingston 1984; 1998; Baier 1991; Merrill 2015; Matson 2017) that see Hume's discourse, from the very start, as deeply Socratic, designed not merely to elucidate principles, but to draw the sympathetic reader into a drama of inquiry—which Melzer (2014) associates with pedagogical esotericism. Indeed, Donald Livingston (1998, 17) argues that the "The Dialectic of True and False Philosophy" is an ever-present dynamic in Hume's thought, from the *Treatise* to the *Dialogues*.

CHAPTER 26

Even Homer Nods: My Line-edits to *The Theory of Moral Sentiments*

I n *Philosophy between the Lines: The Lost History of Esoteric Writing*, Arthur Melzer says we should bring a certain disposition to the text of a great author. We assume that the author "is… correct in all the major aspects of his thinking and also in perfect control of all the major aspects of his writing" (p. 296). It is provisional only, but the more seriously we take an author, the more we resist rejecting the assumption.

In reading TMS, I resist finding flaws. However, even Homer nods. That is, even the wisest and most perspicacious authors make mistakes.

It is proper to suspect the hero-worshipper of putting his hero on a pedestal and reasoning away problems and failings. In presenting himself as exegete—one who expounds on what is in the text —the hero-worshipper is accused of being an eisegete—one who sees things in the text that aren't there.

The very phrase "hero-worshipper" implies overdoing it. One should not be a hero-worshipper. On the other hand, one should not be too afraid of being accused of being a hero-worshipper.

Were the Adam Smith of January 1790 able, transtemporally, to access me now in 2023 for feedback on TMS before finalizing the work, and were I able to return local line-edits, there are a few I would suggest, enumerated below. As these matters presuppose textual intensity on the part of the reader, I here present the suggested changes with minimal explanation, leaving it to the reader to explore their merits.

Some moments in TMS have prompted conjectures of Smith partaking in esoteric writing; some are listed in chapter 24. I am sufficiently open to seeing the TMS items listed there as ironic or sly to refrain from suggesting that Smith revise any of them.

I have not thought much about changes beyond local line-edits, such as changes in arrangement and terminology. Sometimes —but only sometimes—I feel that Smith was too subtle and should have spoon-fed more. It seems thus far that he may have overestimated posterity.

Item 1. The first line-edit concerns Smith's presentation of propriety in connection with the word *mediocrity* (TMS 27.1–2), a word that I think is best reserved (in Smith's moral theory) to signifying the praiseworthy region within a vice/virtue/vice frame (such as cowardice/courage/presumptuous rashness, TMS 270-1.12), as I discussed in chapter 2. At minimum, I would propose that Smith change "This mediocrity, however, in which the point of propriety consists, is different in different passions" (TMS 27.2) to: "This mediocrity, however, which is bound on every side by a point of propriety, is different for different passions." In conjunction with this change, I would suggest that at 243.14, Smith change "the point of propriety" to something like "the point of perfect propriety." I have explained this change in chapter 2.

I am inclined to regard the unclarity of Item 1 as a "Homer

nods" moment. The snarl does not give me much pause about how I interpret Smith on propriety and virtue, nor am I much puzzled that such an unclarity could have occurred and persisted. Item 2 is also fairly minor:

> **Item 2.** In Section III of Part Two, Smith provides a wonderful discussion of the influence of luck on moral sentiment. He sets up a conundrum over our "irregularity of sentiment," namely, letting luck, by way of results, influence our moral sentiments, while we all will say that, should we know intention and the will, then that alone should determine moral sentiments; results, and hence luck, should play no role. Smith's resolution of the conundrum is that we don't in fact know intention/will, and we must turn to results, which inevitably involve luck, as a signal. I would advise Smith to state the resolution a bit more clearly, as I just did. At 108.6, I would suggest that he insert "well informed and" after the "were" when he writes: "if the sentiments of mankind were either altogether candid and equitable, or even perfectly consistent with themselves."

Item 3, however, is the one moment in TMS that continues to disturb me.

> **Item 3.** When Smith distinguishes between virtues having loose, vague, and indeterminate rules and the virtue that has precise and accurate rules, he says something about the latter that I find very peculiar: "The rules of [commutative] justice are accurate in the highest degree, and admit of no exceptions or

modifications *but such as may be ascertained as accurate-ly as the rules themselves*, and which generally, indeed, flow from the very same principles with them" (TMS 175.10, italics added). Smith's remark about "exceptions and modifications" is the part that troubles me. He does not provide an illustration of any such exception or modification, so there is not much for us to go on.

The basic precept of commutative justice is to abstain from what is another's, or not mess with other people's stuff. I understand why he would suggest that the rules of that precept are much more precise and accurate than the rules of other virtues. And I understand why, in rare cases of emergency and so on (I'm thinking of equal-equal jural relations, as, I think, Smith is at this point in the text), one should violate the precept—that is, why one should mess with someone else's stuff. Furthermore, I understand why, in a broad sense, rolling up to universal benevolence, the warrants for an allegiance to commutative justice would also be those for the exceptions. But Smith here seems to suggest that such exceptions "may be ascertained as accurately as the rules themselves." That does not make sense to me. If he means, implicitly, "may be ascertained *by a God-like beholder*," I guess we could go along with the remark. But the whole point of the presentation is to distinguish between precise-and-accurate and loose-vague-and-indeterminate as concerns normal human beings, so suddenly shifting to the capacities of a God-like being would be very incongruous and, so far as I can see, without purpose. I just do not get why he makes the remark.

My suggestion to Smith would be to change the sentence to something like (I italicize what is changed): "The rules of justice are accurate in the highest degree, and admit of no exceptions but such as *might be necessary in only extreme and unusual circumstances and which*, indeed, flow from the very same principles with them." (Notice here, by the way, that I have also dropped "modifications," which differs from "exceptions" in ways that in the sentence exacerbate confusion.)

Item 4. Smith writes: "The first sense of the word [that is, justice] coincides with what Aristotle and the Schoolmen call commutative justice, and with what Grotius calls the *justitia expletrix*, which consists in abstaining from what is another's, and in doing voluntarily whatever we can with propriety be forced to do" (TMS 269.10). I have two issues here. Is it true that both Aristotle and "the Schoolmen" called something "commutative justice" and, more importantly, if they did (and Aquinas's Latin makes it reasonable to maintain that he did), did that correspond to what Smith means by commutative justice? I am doubtful that Aquinas's "commutative justice" corresponds neatly to Smith's, so I would suggest that Smith pause over that matter.

Second, Smith says that his commutative justice "consists in abstaining from what is another's, and in doing voluntarily whatever we can with propriety be forced to do." I think that is basically fine, provided that we are focused on equal-equal jural relations, and the paragraph is, I think, focused upon such. But troubles would arise if the reader extends the sentence to superior-inferior jural relations. I suggest that Smith add "accordingly" (that is, according to the precept of abstaining from what is another's) to make the ending: "whatever we can with propriety accordingly be forced to do." That avoids the hazard of stretching commutative justice to include obedience to any governmental law that can with propriety be enforced.

Item 5. In expositing Smith's tri-layered justice, I have denominated the third sense of justice, which he says is "still more extensive than either of the former" (TMS 270.10), estimative justice, which is estimating objects properly (and hence acting accordingly). Smith writes: "In this last sense, what is called justice means the same thing with exact and perfect propriety of conduct" (TMS 270.10). But, to my mind, the phrasing "means the same thing with" mildly suggests that when it comes to less-than-perfect conduct the notion of estimative justice becomes inapplicable. I would suggest that he reword to: "In this last sense, perfect justice implies exact and perfect propriety of conduct."

Item 6. Smith writes: "Nature, accordingly, has endowed him [man], not only with a desire of being approved of, but with a desire of being what ought to be approved of; or of being what he himself approves of in other men" (TMS 117.7). Occasionally these words have been quoted (see the treatment of Arthur Prior in Klein 2018) to suggest that Smith maintains a sameness of the following two things: (1) a desire on Jim's part of "being what he himself approves of in other men," and (2) a desire

on Jim's part of "being what ought to be approved of."
To forestall such erroneous reading and representation
of Smith, I would suggest inserting "he feels," making
"what he feels ought to be approved of." Likewise, where
Smith writes: "What is agreeable to our moral faculties,
is fit, and right, and proper to be done" (TMS 165.5), I
would suggest inserting "what we feel is" before "fit."

Item 7. The final item is more diffusive and pertains to
something that Smith may have been guarded or esoteric about, namely, the non-foundationalism of his ethics. Were Smith to want to make non-foundationalism
more pronounced, he might have highlighted at 159.8
and 319–320.6–7 how "particular instances" and "general rules" each influence the formation of the other, in
a bi-directional (or spiraling) way, rather than giving so
much more emphasis (at those moments, anyway) to the
influence that particular instances have on the formation of general rules. Also, sometimes he speaks of the
"origin" or "first" event of a process, when he might have
given more of a flavor of picking up in a process under-
way (e.g., the "first" source and "originally" at 188.3; "first"
perceptions" at 320.7; "originally" at 320.8).

In *The Study of Man*, Michael Polanyi (1959, 96) explained that
reverence is a vital tool in the thinker's toolkit. To illustrate, he
posited reverence toward a particular historical figure: Napoleon.
That was to make a point about the hazards of reverence. Heroes
are fallible. Even Homer nods.

CHAPTER 27

You Are a Soul

The original version appeared at the Independent Institute blog The Beacon and was subtitled: Dedicated to the vital spirit of David Theroux.

The ontology of the human being is elusive. But let's say: You are a soul and you own your person.

The soul and the person together constitute the human being. It is also apt, of course, to say you are a human being. But here I use "you" to address just you the soul, to jolt us into a way of thinking.

Souls and persons are one-to-one, so it is natural that "human being" be signified as either "soul" or "person" each serving, according to my formulation, as a synecdoche for the human being.

Where does the person end and the soul begin? I don't know. By "person" I mean more than your body. By "person" I mean something like body and mind. Is the will also part of the person? I don't know. In fact, I am inclined to say that soul has a will and the person has a will. The two wills are related but not one and the same. The ontology remains elusive. But let's say, you are a soul and you own your person.

Here are some implications and thoughts:

1. Each soul enjoys a special knowledge and control over its person. David Hume (2007, 314) wrote of "the fix'd and constant advantages of the mind and body." Likewise, David Friedman (1994) writes

(nine times!) of your person as your "natural property." Since everyone owns his or her person, no one is propertyless.

2. Your person is certainly a unique form of property; it differs from other forms of property. But the most important facet of property applies perfectly to your person: It is something of yours that jural equals are not to mess with. And when government messes with your person, we call it a violation of liberty.

3. You cannot render your person to another human being, and in that sense you cannot alienate your person. In affirming that your person is your property, we hold that alienability is not a necessary feature of property.

4. The only way to abolish all private property would be to annihilate humankind.

5. There is not and never has been such a thing as a slaveowner. Slaveholders do not own the slaves they hold. Slaves own themselves. Slaveholders violate that ownership.

6. For practically everything you enjoy in life, you engage in home production. Your person must interact with digital sources to complete the production of entertainment; your person must interact with the spectacle to enjoy the ball game; your person must interact with your fellows to produce sympathy and communion. The part played by your person in producing every one of your experiences is not merely a "receiving" part, but often a

large part, because so much depends on your person's attitude and aptitudes. That is especially so
for the highest things in your world.

7. Every soul owns its person, and a person is a sort
    of capital good, so every soul is a capitalist. You
    are endowed with what Gary Becker called human
    capital.

8. The demarcating of capital and labor is less clear
    than people usually suppose, since labor is but
    application of your capital, your person, with all of
    its knowledge, abilities, and virtues.

9. Your person is worth a lot to you. It is a valuable
    piece of property. Seeing each's person as wealth,
    we may understand that wealth holdings through-
    out society are more equal than usually reported.

10. When it comes to the doings of your person, some-
    one is watching. That someone is you.

11. You are a principal, and, in your person, you have
    an agent. Your agent is not altogether reliable in
    advancing your interest.

12. You are a constituent of the whole of humankind,
    and, in your person, you have a representative.

13. When your lips form words, and speech comes
    from your mouth, you speak only in as much as
    your person represents you faithfully and accurate-
    ly.

14. You want to commune with other souls. You can
    scarcely do so directly, but must deal with their
    agents or representatives. Adam Smith wrote,

"Frankness and openness conciliate confidence" (TMS 337.28).

15. You and your person are joined. A source of joy is friendship with your person.

16. You have knowledge that your person does not. Assume that the knowledge asymmetries between you and your person are too substantial to ever assume away.

17. You can believe that all souls are good; it is persons that are ever bad. In Swedish, there is a knock that literally means "crunch ball"—*knasboll*. But the Swedish idiom is, "*Din* knasboll!," "*Your* crunch ball." They do not say, "*Du* knasboll!," as Americans might say "*You* jerk!" The idiom is like saying: *Your* crunch ball is acting up. Get him under control!

18. Those who know you regard your person as a symbol of you. Their accessing of your beauty is heightened by every refinement of the symbol.

19. If you also believe that the soul passes out of existence when the person does, you would scarcely ever wish death upon a person, because the soul would die, too. Exceptions could come when the person is a clear and present danger to others.

It is useful and agreeable to think of yourself as a soul that owns its person. It is also useful and agreeable to think that there is a universal benevolent beholder of the whole. On that further notion, we have other implications:

20. Pleasing the universal benevolent beholder provides a framework for ethics. Virtue corresponds

to cooperation with that beholder.

21. The beholder has called each of us to be one of her vicegerents, according to Adam Smith. If you answer the call, you assume a lifetime office of vicegerency. The beholder calls us to make a becoming use of that office, to make a beautiful career.

22. Not only is your person a symbol of you, but, at each moment, the conduct of your person is a symbol of your person's entire performance and character. That lifework strives to signal virtue.

23. Because of the special knowledge and control that each soul has over its person, and because each individual is a part of the whole, ethics authorizes one to focus on his or her local interests, because that is where his or her efforts are most effective and most reliably good. The governmentalization of social affairs is, by and large, frowned on by the beholder, because it makes efforts less reliably good and less effective—indeed, often terrible and inhumane. The governmentalization of social affairs tends to elevate people who are not very virtuous, and to smother us in their baseness and corruption.

It is also useful and agreeable to pattern your thoughts along the lines of benevolent monotheism, that each of us is made by God, and in his image. That too has implications.

CHAPTER 28

Come Together in Adam Smith

I support a classical liberal worldview. I call to social democrats and conservatives alike: Be fair. Let us treat one another like fellow Smithians and come together in Adam Smith.

Adam Smith said we judge under the guidance of exemplars. That is a central principle of *The Theory of Moral Sentiments*. All moral sentiment, that is, all approval or approbation of human conduct, involves a sympathy. Sympathy with whom? Most of all, with moral exemplars as taken into our breast.

Exemplars exemplify virtue in particular instances. Smith gave us particular instances in abundance, by writing two of humankind's greatest works, as well as a few essays—about 1600 pages' worth. We work with Smith's sentences in developing and reforming our sensibilities about what our duties are and how we best fulfill them. Smith generously gave us a moral exemplar.

Smith is our best exemplar, better than any in the nineteenth and twentieth centuries. We need to work our way back to Adam Smith. He propositioned that every case of moral approval be subject to a query.

For example, Hank approves of Jim's action. Samantha asks: Hank, wherein do you find sympathy for your approval of Jim's action? Hank must be ready to lead Samantha to his exemplar, Jean-Jacques (an exemplar with whom Hank finds sympathy). The procedure prompts Hank and Samantha to talk about how Jean-Jacques sees matters like that of Jim's action.

When Hank and Samantha come together in Jean-Jacques,

Samantha may then say, "Sorry, I think Jean-Jacques is all wet on the matter." "Well, Samantha," Hank replies, "wherein do you find sympathy for that disapproval of Jean-Jacques?" Samantha answers: "In Ludwig" (Samantha's exemplar). Now the conversation grows to the matter of Ludwig's view of Jean-Jacques's view of matters like that of Jim's action. By layers, the procedure opens us up to different views of things.

Hank may then take issue with Ludwig's view. "Oh, Samantha, you cannot slavishly follow Ludwig, your Master and Exemplar!" And Hank is right, of course.

In referring to Ludwig, Samantha does not so much identify the one with whom she finds sympathy, but characterizes that one in a way that Hank will find meaningful. The one with whom Samantha finds sympathy is the man within the breast, a figurative being she has developed during her life. By referring to Ludwig, she gives Hank a flavor of her man within the breast, as concerns matters like Jim's action.

"Well, Samantha," Hank might say, "even though your man within the breast resembles Ludwig in matters like Jim's action, my man in the breast does not. Mine resembles Jean-Jacques, so where does that leave us?"

Adam Smith urges them on. He would say to Hank:

> Hank, your man within the breast is the representative of an impartial, super-knowledgeable, benevolent spectator. And Samantha's man within the breast, too, is a representative of the same spectator. Now, as you and Samantha have not found sympathy in the matter of Jim's action, there must be a problem in the representations developed within your breasts. We all know that

> none of us has full or direct access to the impartial spec-
> tator, that each of our man-within-the-breasts is merely
> human. Talk with Samantha about how you think the
> impartial spectator would look at your man within the
> breast vis-à-vis her man within the breast.

Smith's proposition is to knowingly buy into two procedures.
First, we see all moral approval as involving a sympathy. Second,
we mutually seek a common standpoint to address our moral differences. The procedures prompt us to come together to enter into
each other's ways of seeing, to tolerate our differences, to consider
that maybe our man within the breast should change somewhat.
In embracing Smith's proposition, we better accommodate our differences, maybe resolve them to some extent.

One of the most remarkable things about Smith is how universally he is beloved. Economists, political scientists, sociologists,
psychologists, historians, philosophers, and humanities scholars
love him. Believers and skeptics love him. Social democrats, conservatives, and classical liberals love him.

Smith accommodates such diversity by bypassing some of the
pitfalls that divide us. His proposition bypasses, for instance, the
absolutism-relativism dichotomy: The impartial spectator is universal, but that which she surveys is rich and variegated, the historical tree of particularistic human contexts; she approves of "steal
the bread" at one branch and not at another. The survey is universal, and it condemns many social customs—Smith condemned
many. But rules are formulated in relation to situations to which
they pertain. By narrowing the set of situations, we make the rule
more "absolute." By widening the set so as to take in situations in
which we approve of exceptions to the rule, we make the rule only
presumptive, or "relative" to the situation within the set.

By receiving one another as good Smithians, we overcome stereotypes. We come together to improve affairs of common concern.

References

Anonymous. 1764. *An Essay in Vindication of the Continental Colonies of America, From a Censure of Mr Adam Smith, in His Theory of Moral Sentiments*. Becket and De Hondt.

Aron, Raymond. 1994. *In Defense of Political Reason*, edited by D. J. Mahoney. Rowman & Littlefield.

Asher, Kendra H. 2022. Was David Hume a Racist? Interpreting Hume's Infamous Footnote (Part I). *Economic Affairs* 42 (2): 225–239.

Aydinonat, N. Emrah. 2008. *The Invisible Hand in Economics: How Economists Explain Unintended Social Consequences*. Routledge.

Baier, Annette. 1991. *A Progress of Sentiments: Reflections on Hume's Treatise*. Harvard University Press.

Baillie, John. 1747. *An Essay on the Sublime*. R. Dodsley.

Bentham, Jeremy. 1787. *Defence of Usury*. Paine and Foss.

Berlin, Isaiah. 1969. Two Concepts of Liberty. In *Four Essays on Liberty*: 118–172. Oxford University Press.

Berry, C. 1974. Adam Smith's Considerations on Language. *Journal of the History of Ideas* 35 (1): 130–138.

Bonica, Mark J., and Daniel B. Klein. 2021. Adam Smith on Reputation, Commutative Justice, and Defamation Laws. *Journal of Economic Behavior & Organization* 184: 788–803.

Boudreaux, Donald J. 2019. Looking Back–With Enormous Gratitude–Over the Past 61 Years. *Cafe Hayek*, September 10.

———. 2020. Today's Relevance of Adam Smith's Wealth of Nations. *The Independent Review* 24 (4): 487–497.

———. 2022. Also Misunderstands Comparative Advantage. *Cafe Hayek*, March 26.

Brown, Vivienne. 1994. *Adam Smith's Discourse: Canonicity, Commerce, and Conscience*. Routledge.

Brubaker, Lauren. 2006. Does the 'Wisdom of Nature' Need Help? In *New Voices on Adam Smith*, edited by Leonidas Montes and Eric Schliesser, 330–372. Routledge.

Bryce, J, ed. 1983. Introduction, in Adam Smith: *Lectures on Rhetoric and Belles Lettres*, 1–37. Oxford University Press.

Buckle, Stephen. 1991. *Natural Law and the Theory of Property: Grotius to Hume*. Clarendon Press.

Burke, Edmund. 1957. *A Note-Book of Edmund Burke*, edited by H.V.F. Somerset. Cambridge University Press.

Burke, Edmund. 1958. *The Correspondence of Edmund Burke.* Volume 1: April 1744–June 1768, edited by T.W. Copeland. Cambridge University Press.

———. 1982 [1756]. *A Vindication of Natural Society*, edited by F.N. Pagano. Liberty Fund.

———. 1992. *Further Reflections on the Revolution in France*, edited by D.E. Ritchie. Liberty Fund.

———. 1999. *Selected Works of Edmund Burke*, Volume 1, edited by F. Canavan and E. J. Payne. Liberty Fund.

Capaldi, Nicholas, and Gordon Lloyd. 2016. *Liberty and Equality in Political Economy; From Locke versus Rousseau to the Present.* Edward Elgar.

Caplan, Bryan. 2017. The Consumer Gratitude Heuristic. *EconLog*, May 1.

———. 2022. The Final Freedom. *Bet On It*, June 23.

Carmichael, Gershom. 2002. *Natural Rights on the Threshold of the Scottish Enlightenment: The Writings of Gershom Carmichael*, edited by J. Moore, translated by M. Silverthorne. Liberty Fund.

Cass, Oren. 2022a. Searching for Capitalism in the Wreckage of Globalization. *American Compass*, March 9.

———. 2022b. The Conservative Confusion on Globalization. *National Review*, March 16.

Christopher, Emma. 2006. *Slave Ship Sailors and Their Captive Cargoes, 1730–1807.* Cambridge University Press.

Clark, J. R., and Dwight R. Lee. 2017. Econ 101 Morality: The Amiable, the Mundane, and the Market. *Econ Journal Watch* 14 (1): 61–76.

Clarkson, Thomas. 1808. *The History of the Rise, Progress, & Accomplishment of the Abolition of the African Slave-Trade, by the British Parliament*, vol. 2. Longman, Hurst, Rees, and Orme.

Constant, Benjamin. 1819. The Liberty of Ancients Compared with That of Moderns.

Continetti, Matthew. 2022. *The Right: The Hundred-Year War for American Conservatism.* Hachette.

Craig, David. 2012. The Origins of 'Liberalism' in Britain: The Case of The Liberal. *Historical Research* 85 (229): 469–487.

Dascal, M. 2006. Adam Smith's Theory of Language. In *The Cambridge Companion to Adam Smith*, edited by Knud Haakonssen, 79–111. Cambridge University Press.

DelliSanti, Dylan. 2021. The Dynamism of Liberalism: An Esoteric Interpretation of Adam Smith. *Journal of Economic Behavior & Organization* 184: 717–726.

Diesel, Jonathan H. 2020. Two Superiors, Two Jural Relationships in Adam Smith. *Adam Smith Review* 12.

———. 2021. Adam Smith on Usury: An Esoteric Reading. *Journal of Economic Behavior & Organization* 184: 727–738.

Diesel, Jonathan and Daniel B. Klein. 2021. A Call to Embrace Jural Dualism. *Economic Affairs* 41: 442–457.

Drylie, Scott. 2020. Professional Scholarship from 1893 to 2020 on Adam Smith's Views on School Funding: A Heterodox Examination. *Econ Journal Watch* 17 (2): 350–391.

———. 2021. Adam Smith on Schooling: A Classical Liberal Rereading. *Journal of Economic Behavior & Organization* 184: 748–770.

Edwards, Thomas. 1646. *Gangræna: Or a Catalogue and Discovery of Many of the Errors, Heresies, Blasphemies and Pernicious Practices of the Sectaries of This Time.* Ralph Smith.

Field, Alexander J. 2004. *Altruistically Inclined? The Behavioral Sciences, Evolutionary Theory, and the Origins of Reciprocity.* Ann Arbor, Michigan: University of Michigan Press.

Forman-Barzilai, Fonna. 2010. *Adam Smith and the Circles of Sympathy: Cosmopolitanism and Moral Theory.* Cambridge University Press.

Friedman, David. 1994. A Positive Account of Property Rights. *Social Philosophy and Policy* 11 (2): 1–16.

Goldberg, Jonah. 2018. *Suicide of the West: How the Rebirth of Tribalism, Populism, Nationalism, and Identity Politics Is Destroying American Democracy.* Crown Forum.

Grampp, William D. 2000. What Did Adam Smith Mean by the Invisible Hand? *Journal of Political Economy* 108 (3): 441–465.

Griswold, Charles L. 1999. *Adam Smith and the Virtues of Enlightenment.* Cambridge University Press.

Grotius, Hugo. 2005. *The Rights of War and Peace* (Three vols.), edited by Richard Tuck, translated by J. Barbeyrac. Liberty Fund.

Grotius, Hugo. 2011 [1853]. *Grotius on the Rights of War and Peace.* An Abridged Translation, edited by W. Whewell. Lawbook Exchange Ltd.

Haakonssen, Knud. 1981. *The Science of a Legislator: The Natural Jurisprudence of David Hume and Adam Smith.* Cambridge University Press.

Haidt, Jonathan. 2012. *The Righteous Mind: Why Good People Are Divided by Politics and Religion.* Pantheon.

Hallam, Henry. 1839. *Introduction to the Literature of Europe in the Fifteenth, Sixteenth and Seventeenth Centuries.* Harper & Brothers, Publishers.

———. 2011. *The Constitutional History of England from the Accession of Henry VII to the Death of George II.* Cambridge University Press.

Harrison, Peter. 2011. Adam Smith and the History of the Invisible Hand. *Journal of the History of Ideas* 72 (1): 29–49.

Hay, Daisy. 2008. Liberals, Liberales, and The Liberal: A Reassessment. *European Romantic Review* 19 (4): 307–320.

Hayek, Friedrich A. 1948. *Individualism and Economic Order.* University of Chicago Press.

———. 1960. *The Constitution of Liberty.* University of Chicago Press.

———. 1976. *Law, Legislation, and Liberty, Vol 2: The Mirage of Social Justice.* University of Chicago Press.

———. 1978. The Atavism of Social Justice. In *New Studies in Philosophy, Politics, Economics and the History of Ideas*, 57–68. University of Chicago Press.

———. 1979. The Three Sources of Human Values. In *Law, Legislation and Liberty, Vol. 3: The Political Order of a Free People*, 153–76. University of Chicago Press.

———. 1988. *The Fatal Conceit: The Errors of Socialism*. University of Chicago Press.

Hume, David. 1983. *The History of England from the Invasion of Julius Caesar to the Revolution in 1688*, edited by W.B. Todd. 6 vols. Liberty Fund.

———. 1987. *Essays, Moral, Political, and Literary*, ed. E. F. Miller. Liberty Fund.

———. 1998. *An Enquiry Concerning the Principles of Morals*, edited by T. L. Beauchamp. Clarendon Press.

———. 2000. *An Enquiry Concerning Human Understanding*, edited by T. L. Beauchamp. Clarendon Press.

———. 2007. *A Treatise of Human Nature*, edited by D. F. Norton and M. J. Norton. 2 vols. Oxford University Press.

Hutcheson, Francis. 2007. *A Short Introduction to Moral Philosophy*, edited by L. Turco. Liberty Fund.

Kames, Lord. 1762. *Elements of Criticism*, edited by P. Jones. 2 vols. Liberty Fund.

Kennedy, Gavin. 2009. Adam Smith and the Invisible Hand: From Metaphor to Myth. *Econ Journal Watch* 6 (2): 239–262.

Klein, Daniel B. 2014. Review of Dennis Rasmussen, The Problems and Promise of Commercial Society: Adam Smith's Response to Rousseau. *Adam Smith Review* 7: 323–329.

———. 2017. Glimpses of David Hume. *Econ Journal Watch* 14 (3): 474–487.

———. 2018. Dissing *The Theory of Moral Sentiments*: Twenty-Six Critics, from 1765 to 1949. *Econ Journal Watch* 15 (2): 201–254.

———. 2019. Is It Just to Pursue Honest Income? *Economic Affairs* 39: 400–409.

———. 2020. Christianity to Liberalism: An Interview with Daniel Klein. *Svensk Tidskrift*, August 28.

———. 2021. Commutative, Distributive, and Estimative Justice in Adam Smith. *Adam Smith Review* 12: 82–102.

Klein, Daniel B., and Kendra H. Asher. 2022. Adam Smith's Unmerited Censure: Revisiting a Satirical 1764 Pamphlet on Slavery. *American Political Thought* 11 (1): 48–72.

Klein, Daniel B., and Donald J. Boudreaux. 2017. The 'Trade Deficit': Defective Language, Deficient Thinking. *EconLib*. June 15.

Klein, Daniel B., and Michael J. Clark. 2010. Direct and Overall Liberty: Areas and Extent of Disagreement. *Reason Papers* 32, Fall: 41–66.

Klein, Daniel B., and Brandon Lucas. 2011. In a Word or Two, Placed in the Middle: The Invisible Hand in Adam Smith's Tomes. *Economic Affairs* 31 (1): 43–52.

Klein, Daniel B., and Erik W. Matson. 2020. Mere-Liberty in David Hume. In *A Companion to David Hume*, edited by by Moris Polanco, 125–160. Universidad Francisco Marroquin.

Klein, Daniel B., Erik W. Matson, and Colin Doran. 2018. The Man Within the Breast, the Supreme Impartial Spectator, and Other Impartial Spectators in Adam Smith's 'Theory of Moral Sentiments.' *History of European Ideas* 44 (8): 1153–1168.

Klein, Daniel B., and Dominic Pino, eds. 2022. *Edmund Burke and the Perennial Battle, 1789–1797.* Fraser Institute/CL Press.

Knox, Norman. 1961. *The Word Irony and Its Context, 1500–1755.* Duke University Press.

Kondik, Kyle, J. Miles Coleman, and Larry J. Sabato. 2021. New Initiative Explores Deep, Persistent Divides Between Biden and Trump Voters. *Sabato's Crystal Ball*, September 30.

Leonhard, Jörn. 2004. From European Liberalism to the Languages of Liberalisms: The Semantics of Liberalism. *European Comparison. Redescriptions: Yearbook of Political Thought and Conceptual History* 8: 17–51.

Lewis, C.S. 1944. *The Abolition of Man.* Zondervan.

Lewis, David K. 1969. *Convention: A Philosophical Study.* Cambridge, MA: Harvard University Press.

Livingston, Donald W. 1984. *Hume's Philosophy of Common Life.* Chicago: University of Chicago Press.

———. 1998. *Philosophical Melancholy and Delirium: Hume's Pathology of Philosophy.* Chicago: University of Chicago Press.

Macfie, A.L. 1967. The Moral Justification of Free Enterprise. *Scottish Journal of Political Economy* 14 (1): 1–11.

Macfie, Alec. 1971. The Invisible Hand of Jupiter. *Journal of the History of Ideas* 32 (4): 595–599.

Maitland, Frederic William. 1875. *A Historical Sketch of Liberty and Equality.* Indianapolis: Liberty Fund.

Martin, Thomas. 2014. The Sunbathing Beggar and Fighting Kings: Diogenes the Cynic and Alexander the Great in Adam Smith's Theory of Moral Sentiments. *Adam Smith Review* 8: 217–240.

Matson, Erik W. 2017. The Dual Account of Reason and the Spirit of Philosophy in Hume's *Treatise. Hume Studies* 43 (2), 29–56.

———. 2018. Adam Smith's Humean Attitude towards Science: Illustrated by 'The History of Astronomy.' *Adam Smith Review* 11: 265–280.

———. 2021. A Dialectical Reading of Adam Smith on Wealth and Happiness. *Journal of Economic Behavior & Organization* 184: 826–836.

———. 2022a. The Edifying Discourses of Adam Smith: Focalism, Commerce, and Serving the Common Good. *Journal of the History of Economic Thought*, forthcoming.

———. 2022b. What Is Liberal about Adam Smith's 'Liberal Plan'? *Southern Economic Journal*, forthcoming.

Matson, Erik W., and Colin Doran. 2017. The Elevated Imagination: Contemplation and Action in David Hume and Adam Smith. *Journal of Scottish Philosophy* 15 (1): 27–45.

Matson, Erik W., Colin Doran, and Daniel B. Klein. 2019. Hume and Smith on Utility, Agreeableness, Propriety, and Moral Approval. *History of European Ideas* 45 (5): 675–704.

Matson, Erik W., and Daniel B. Klein. 2022. Convention without Convening: Hume's Marvelous Innovation. *Constitutional Political Economy* 33 (1): 1–24.

McCloskey, Deirdre N. 2019. *Why Liberalism Works: How True Liberal Values Produce a Freer, More Equal, Prosperous World for All.* Yale University Press.

McCloskey, Deirdre N., and Art Carden. 2020. *Leave Me Alone and I'll Make You Rich: How the Bourgeois Deal Enriched the World.* University of Chicago Press.

McCloskey, Deirdre N. 2006. *The Bourgeois Virtues: Ethics for an Age of Commerce.* The University of Chicago Press.

———. 2010. *Bourgeois Dignity: Why Economics Can't Explain the Modern World.* University of Chicago Press.

———. 2016. *Bourgeois Equality: How Ideas, Not Capital or Institutions, Enriched the World.* University of Chicago Press.

McCulloch, John Ramsay. 1824. Political Economy. In *Supplement to the Fourth, Fifth, and Sixth Editions of the Encyclopedia Britannica with Preliminary Dissertations of the History of the Sciences.* Archibald Constable and Company; Hurst, Robinson, and Company.

McGilchrist, Iain. 2009. *The Master and His Emissary: The Divided Brain and the Making of the Western World.* Yale University Press.

McVickar, John. [1825] 1966. *Outlines of Political Economy.* Kelly.

Melzer, Arthur M. 2014. *Philosophy Between the Lines: The Lost History of Esoteric Writing.* Princeton University Press.

Merrill, Thomas W. 2015. Hume's Socratism. *Review of Politics* 77: 23–45.

Millar, John. 2006. *The Origin of the Distinction of Ranks*, edited by A. Garrett. Liberty Fund.

Minowitz, Peter. 1993. *Profits, Priests, and Princes: Adam Smith's Emancipation of Economics from Politics and Religion.* Stanford University Press.

———. 2004. Adam Smith's Invisible Hands. *Econ Journal Watch* 1 (3): 381–412.

Munger, Mike. 2018. Can Libertarianism Be a Governing Philosophy? *Law & Liberty*, March 1.

Murphy, Jon, and Andrew Humphries. 2021. His Memory Has Misled Him? Two Supposed Errors in Adam Smith's Theory of Moral Sentiments. *Journal of Economic Behavior & Organization* 184: 771–80.

Nefftzer, Auguste. 1883. Liberalism. In *Cyclopedia of Political Science, Political Economy, and of the Political History of the United States*, edited by John Joseph Lalor, vol. 2, 759–66. Melbert B. Cary.

Newton, John. 1962. *The Journal of a Slave Trader 1750–1754, With Newton's Thoughts upon the African Slave Trade*, edited by B. Martin and M. Spurell. Epworth Press.

Oslington, Paul. 2012. God and Market: Adam Smith's Invisible Hand. *Journal of Business Ethics* 108 (4): 429–38.

Pack, Spencer J. 1995. Adam Smith's Unnaturally Natural (Nonetheless Naturally Unnatural) Use of the Word Natural. In *The Classical Tradition in Economic Thought: Perspectives on the History of Economic Thought*, vol. 11, edited by Ingrid H. Rima, 31–42. Edward Elgar.

Paley, William. 1802. *Natural Theology: Or, Evidences of the Existence and Attributes of the Deity.* John Morgan.

Palmer, R.R., and J. Colton. 2007. *A History of the Modern World.* 10th ed. McGraw-Hill.

Parfit, Derek. 1998. Why Anything? Why This? *London Review of Books* 20 (3), February 5.

Peart, Sandra J., and David M. Levy. 2005. *The 'Vanity of the Philosopher': From Equality to Hierarchy in Post-Classical Economics.* University of Michigan Press.

Pinker, Steven. 2002. *The Blank Slate: The Modern Denial of Human Nature.* Penguin Books.

Pino, Dominic. 2022. The Inevitability of Special Interests in Government Intervention. *National Review,* March 20.

Pocock, J. G. A. 1983. Cambridge Paradigms and Scotch Philosophers: A Study of the Relations between the Civic Humanist and the Civil Jurisprudential Interpretation of Eighteenth-Century Social Thought. In *Wealth and Virtue: The Shaping of Political Economy in the Scottish Enlightenment*, edited by I. Hont and M. Ignatieff, 235–252. Cambridge University Press.

Polanyi, Karl. 1944. *The Great Transformation: The Political and Economic Origins of Our Time.* Rinehart & Co.

Polanyi, Michael. 1959. *The Study of Man.* University of Chicago Press.

Rediker, Marcus. 2007. *The Slave Ship: A Human History.* Penguin Books.

Robinson, John A., and J. Robert Subrick. 2021. Why Did Smith Suggest a Labor Theory of Value? *Journal of Economic Behavior & Organization* 184: 781–787.

Rosenblatt, Helena. 2018. *The Lost History of Liberalism: From Ancient Rome to the Twenty-First Century.* Princeton University Press.

Ross, Ian Simpson. 2010. *The Life of Adam Smith.* 2nd ed. Oxford University Press.

Rosten, Leo. 1968. *The Joys of Yiddish.* Simon and Schuster.

Rush, Benjamin. 1773. *An Address to the Inhabitants of the British Settlements in America, Upon Slave-Keeping* [to Which Is Appended a Second Pamphlet, Also Attributed to Rush, A Vindication of the Address]. John Dunlap.

Shapiro, J. Salwyn. 1958. *Liberalism: Its Meaning and History.* Van Nostrand.

Simler, Kevin, and Robin Hanson. 2017. *The Elephant in the Brain: Hidden Motives in Everyday Life.* Oxford University Press.

Smith, Adam. [1776] 1976. *An Inquiry into the Nature and Causes of the Wealth of Nations*, edited by R. H. Campbell, A. S. Skinner, and W. B. Todd. Oxford: Oxford University Press. Liberty Fund, 1981.

———. 1976 [1790]. *The Theory of Moral Sentiments*, edited by D. D. Raphael and A. L. Macfie. Oxford University Press. Indianapolis: Liberty Fund, 1982.

———. 1980. *Essays on Philosophical Subjects*, edited by W. P. D. Wightman and J. C. Bryce. Oxford University Press. Reprint: Liberty Fund, 1980.

———. 1982. *Lectures on Jurisprudence,* edited by R.L. Meek, D.D. Raphael, and P.G. Stein. Oxford University Press. Liberty Fund, 1982.

———. 1983. *Lectures on Rhetoric and Belles Lettres,* edited by J.C. Bryce. Oxford: Clarendon Press. Liberty Fund.

Smith, Craig. 2006. *Adam Smith's Political Philosophy: The Invisible Hand and Spontaneous Order.* Routledge.

Sober, Elliott, and David Sloan Wilson. 1998. *Unto Others: The Evolution and Psychology of Unselfish Behavior.* Harvard University Press.

Stephen, James Fitzjames. 1862. Liberalism. *Cornhill Magazine* 5: 70–84.

Stewart, Dugald. 1854. *The Collected Works of Dugald Stewart,* vol. 1: *The Progress of Metaphysical, Ethical, and Political Philosophy since the Revival of Letters in Europe,* edited by W. Hamilton. Constable and Co.

Sumner, Charles. 1860. Speech in Congress. *The Congressional Globe,* June 4. Washington DC.

Tocqueville, Alexis de. 2000. *Democracy in America.* Translated and edited by Harvey Mansfield and Debra Winthrop. University of Chicago Press.

Trenchard, John. 1709. *Natural History of Superstition.* Oxford: A. Baldwin.

Weingast, Barry R. 2020. Persistent Inefficiency: Adam Smith's Theory of Slavery and Its Abolition in Western Europe. *Adam Smith Review* 12: 290–310.

Wilberforce, William. 1797. *A Practical View of the Prevailing Religious System of Professed Christians.* Cadell and Davies.

Wilson, Bart. 2020. *The Property Species: Mine, Yours, and the Human Mind.* Oxford University Press.

Wiltermuth, Scott C., and Chip Heath. 2009. Synchrony and Cooperation. *Psychological Science* 20 (1): 1–5.

Winters, Barbara. 1979. Hume on Reason. *Hume Studies* 5 (1): 20–35.

Zywicki, Todd. 2000. Was Hayek Right about Group Selection After All? *Review of Austrian Economics* 13: 81–95.

Index

self-delusion, 158
Shakespeare, William, 113, 130
Shapiro, J. Salwyn, 133
Simler, Kevin, 156
Simon, Paul, 126
slave trade, slavery, 57–78, 150, 199, 210
slaveholders, as opposed to "slaveown-
        ers", 210
social cohesion, 27, 38
social grammar, 117–18, 21, 26, 106, 174
social justice, 23, 42–43
Society for the Effecting of the Abolition
        of the Slave Trade, 67
Solon, 65
song of death, 59
soul sympathy, 38
spiral, 20, 29, 48, 51, 165, 178, 207; herme-
        neutic, 165
spontaneous order, 120, 123
status quo, presumption of, 80, 144
Stephen, James Fitzjames, 133
Stewart, Dugald, 120, 169
Stratocles, 150
suicide, 66, 199
superior prudence, 19
surprise, 48, 188
suum. See one's own.

Swift, Jonathan, 75
sympathetic deftness, 28, 31, 33, 38
sympathy, 9, 28, 36, 175–76, 183; habitu-
        al, 30; pleasure of mutual, 34, 177–
        78; with man within the breast, 34;
        in modern society, 37–38
synchrony, 175–86
Tao, 71–72
Tertullian, 148
Theroux, David, a dedication to, 209
those we live with, 35
Tierney, Brian, 115
Tocqueville, Alexis de, 139
trade deficit, 85
treason, 114
Trenchard, John, 45
usury laws, 189–90, 198
vicegerents, 167
vulgar prudence, 19
Whewell, William, 148
Wilberforce, William, 68
Wilson, Bart, 95–6
Wiltermuth, Scott C., 175, 184, 185
wonder, 19n2, 48, 84, 188
workmate, 30
workplace, 28, 30

Searchable PDF of this entire book,
with colors in figures,
open access, free:
https://clpress.net/

CL Press

A Fraser Institute Project

https://clpress.net/

Professor Daniel Klein (George Mason University, Economics and
Mercatus Center) and Dr. Erik Matson (Mercatus Center), directors of
the Adam Smith Program at George Mason University, are the editors
and directors of CL Press. CL stands at once for classical liberal and
conservative liberal.

CL Press is a project of the Fraser Institute (Vancouver, Canada).

People:

Dan Klein and **Erik Matson** are the co-editors and executives
of the imprint.

Jane Shaw Stroup is Editorial Advisor, doing especially
copy-editing and text preparation.

An Advisory Board:

Jordan Ballor, *Center for Religion, Culture, and Democracy*
Caroline Breashears, *St. Lawrence Univ.*
Donald Boudreaux, *George Mason Univ.*
Ross Emmett, *Arizona State Univ.*
Knud Haakonssen, *Univ. of St. Andrews*
Björn Hasselgren, *Timbro, Uppsala Univ.*
Karen Horn, *Univ. of Erfurt*
Jimena Hurtado, *Univ. de los Andes*
Nelson Lund, *George Mason Univ.*
Daniel Mahoney, *Assumption Univ.*

Deirdre N. McCloskey, *Univ. of Illinois–Chicago*
Thomas W. Merrill, *American Univ.*
James Otteson, *Univ. of Notre Dame*
Catherine R. Pakaluk, *Catholic Univ. of America*
Sandra Peart, *Univ. of Richmond*
Mario Rizzo, *New York Univ.*
Loren Rotner, *Univ. of Austin*
Marc Sidwell, *New Culture Forum*
Craig Smith, *Univ. of Glasgow*
Emily Skarbek, *Brown Univ.*
David Walsh, *Catholic Univ. of America*
Richard Whatmore, *Univ. of St. Andrews*
Barry Weingast, *Stanford Univ.*
Lawrence H. White, *George Mason Univ.*
Amy Willis, *Liberty Fund*
Bart Wilson, *Chapman Univ.*
Todd Zywicki, *George Mason Univ.*

Why start CL Press?

CL Press publishes good, low-priced work in intellectual history, political theory, political economy, and moral philosophy. More specifically, CL Press explores and advance discourse in the following areas:

* The intellectual history and meaning of liberalism.

* The relationship between liberalism and conservatism.

* The role of religion in disseminating liberal understandings and institutions including: humankind's ethical universalism, the moral equality of souls, the rule of law, religious liberty, the meaning and virtues of economic life.

* The relationship between religion and economic philosophy.

CPSIA information can be obtained
at www.ICGtesting.com
Printed in the USA
LVHW091104230123
737638LV00001B/3